Mother Goose Rhyme Time

People

Kimberly K. Faurot

Illustrated by Steve Cox

Musical Notations by Sara L. Waters

UpstartBooks

Fort Atkinson, Wisconsin

www.upstartbooks.com

Acknowledgments
Saroj Ghoting, Early Literacy Consultant

Special thanks to the following individuals and institutions:
Brad Kruse
Steve Cox
Sara L. Waters
Kristi McNellis
Lyle and JoAnne Faurot
Cathy Norris and the Children's Department staff, past and present,
of the Hedberg Public Library, Janesville, WI
Pat Hall
Carmel Clay Public Library Children's Department, Carmel, IN
Dr. Shirley Fitzgibbons
Jim Peitzman
Ann Denton
St. Paul Public Library, St. Paul, MN
University of Minnesota Libraries

All Highsmith/Upstart staff who worked on this project, including:
Matt Mulder, Publisher
Michelle McCardell, Managing Editor
Heidi Green, Art Director
Joann Lueck, Graphic Designer
Matt Napier, Production Designer
Sandy Harris, Product Development Manager

Published by UpstartBooks
W5527 State Road 106
P.O. Box 800
Fort Atkinson, Wisconsin 53538-0800
1-800-448-4887

Text © Kimberly K. Faurot, 2006
Illustrations © Steve Cox, 2006

The paper used in this publication meets the minimum requirements of American National Standard for Information Science—Permanence of Paper for Printed Library Material. ANSI/NISO Z39.48-1992.

All rights reserved. Printed in the United States of America.
The purchase of this book entitles the individual librarian or teacher to reproduce copies for use in the library or classroom. The reproduction of any part for an entire school system or for commercial use is strictly prohibited. No form of this work may be reproduced or transmitted or recorded without written permission from the publisher.

Contents

Introduction

Each Mother Goose Rhyme Time book is designed as a companion to a large size Mother Goose poster and character set. The books enhance the characters' possibilities by providing brief histories of each rhyme, simple musical notations so the rhymes may be played and sung, and suggestions for successfully incorporating the rhymes into library storytimes or classroom lessons.

Before You Begin

Punch out, laminate, and assemble the character cutouts as directed on the punch-out pages. Create an organized storage system so each poster and its accompanying pieces are easily accessible and safe from damage.

Why Nursery Rhymes?

Researchers have determined that young children who know nursery rhymes have a distinct advantage over those who do not as they embark upon the journey toward literacy (Bryant, Bradley, MacLean, and Crossland 426).

Nursery rhymes specifically foster and enhance:

- Acquisition of new vocabulary and concepts

- Oral language abilities, including the internalization of characteristic speech rhythms and intonation patterns

- Phonological awareness/sensitivity, the ability to recognize that spoken words consist of sound segments

- Sensitivity to and ability to detect rhyme and alliteration

Targeted nursery rhyme activities may additionally be used to help develop memorization skills, narrative skills and sequencing, print motivation, print awareness and tracking, and letter knowledge.

The linguistic routines inherent in nursery rhymes provide opportunities for children to hear sound similarities and differences, consequently developing and enhancing their phonological skills (MacLean, Bryant, and Bradley 277). In turn, phonological awareness is a key factor in eventual mastery of reading and spelling. This awareness of the smaller sounds in words does not develop automatically, in contrast to speech perception abilities, which are typically natural and spontaneous (National Research Council 51–57). Encouraging these phonological skills through introduction to rhyme and alliteration helps establish a foundation for effective decoding, and ultimately is a critical skill for fluent reading later on.

Early Literacy

Nursery rhymes are one of the building blocks of early literacy, a perspective that emphasizes skill development through young children's positive interactions with books and with caregivers, and regular exposure to literacy-rich environments and experiences. Early literacy does not mean teaching actual reading earlier, but laying a firm foundation for reading later on (Zero to Three). As MacLean, Bryant, and Bradley note, "... children acquire phonological awareness a long time before learning to read, through experiences which at the time have nothing to do with reading" (278). Activities such as chewing on and handling books, looking at and pointing to storybook pictures, saying rhymes and singing songs, rudimentary recognition of and interest in letters of the alphabet, and scribbling all help establish a child's preliminary foundation of knowledge about reading and writing long before he or she is developmentally ready to actually read or write. Just as a baby's babbling is a precursor to formal speech, these and other early literacy behaviors are precursors to reading (Project ECLIPSE).

For All Ages

Nursery rhymes are ideal components of programs for very young children, who respond naturally to the verses' engaging meter. The rhymes' brevity makes them well suited to short attention spans, and their bounceable, jumpable, clappable rhythms make them helpful tools in engaging active young listeners.

Despite this natural affinity, many children are not introduced to nursery rhymes as infants or preschoolers, and consequently require formal exposure upon reaching school. As children grow, nursery rhymes can play a shifting yet vital role in their literacy development. Incorporating rhymes into storytimes and activities for older children can establish confidence in "reading" a rhyme that is already comfortable and known; enhance phonological awareness and subsequently reading abilities; and provide a springboard for lessons in such diverse subjects as math, punctuation, creative writing, and history. Comparing the illustrations from various versions of Mother Goose can develop visual literacy, and research techniques may be taught through investigating the rhymes' possible origins. Older children can reminisce about the wording of rhymes that they remember from their own early years, and then compare those versions to the many different adaptations available.

Nursery rhymes are similarly effective in the elementary ESL/ELL (English as a Second Language/English Language Learners) classroom, supplying interesting characters, opportunities for vocabulary development, and plenty of action. The rhymes' natural rhythms help students develop an understanding of English speech cadences and intonation, as they do with very young children just beginning to utilize spoken language. Since most cultures have their own traditional play rhymes and songs, students can share and teach these in their native language to classmates and teachers. Cultural rhymes, games, and songs can also provide an ideal venue for parent/caregiver involvement with a child's class, and for affirming the vital importance of each student's cultural identity. Assignments may include children learning traditional rhymes at home to subsequently share in school or as part of a special presentation for

family members. Parents or caregivers can be invited to attend the class as visiting instructors to teach rhymes and songs from their own childhoods, encouraging appreciation for and recognition of their family's history.

In addition to the rhythms and phonological connections that nursery rhymes help promote, educators recognize that children must be familiar with the rhymes' content and meaning to understand many cultural allusions and references throughout their lives.

How to Use this Book

Utilize the sections of Mother Goose Rhyme Time that work best for you and your storytime group or classroom. Experiment with new ideas and techniques. Practice ahead of time so you feel comfortable with the material and can focus on the audience rather than on trying to remember how you intended to share the rhyme. Consider introducing "Mother Goose Rhyme Time" each week with a Mother Goose puppet or special song to signal what will happen next. For example:

> *(Tune: "The Farmer in the Dell")*
> It's time for Mother Goose
> I've heard she's on the loose!
> She'll bring a rhyme for storytime,
> It's time for Mother Goose!

Each chapter includes the following sections:

Rhyme

A standard version of the nursery rhyme, which matches the poster included in the companion set.

Variants

Alternate wording or versions of the rhyme that are different from the version in this book.

History

A brief historical note about the rhyme's possible origins. Occasionally sharing bits of background information can add to the rhyme's charm and entertainment value for parents and

caregivers as they find themselves inevitably reading it repeatedly with their child! The references may also be used as a familiar and engaging entry to older students' history lessons.

Musical Notation

Simple, storytime-tested melodies for each rhyme, with autoharp/guitar chords. Tunes reflect standard melodies if any are known, and offer straightforward new adaptations for rhymes with obscure historical tunes.

Preparing and Using the Mother Goose Rhyme Time Pieces

A list of the rhyme pieces and the poster are needed for presenting each rhyme, with preliminary preparation and presentation suggestions. For example, before sharing the rhyme, place the poster on an easel so the audience can see it clearly. For some rhymes, pieces may be stacked in reverse order of appearance and hidden out of sight before the audience arrives. Rhyme pieces may be held in the presenter's hands, glued or taped securely to a paint stirrer and held aloft, or affixed to a large Velcro or magnet board. If you wish to incorporate motions or use a musical instrument for accompaniment, point to each piece on the board in turn as you lead the group in the actions or play and sing the song.

Storytime

Ideas for sharing the nursery rhyme as a song or chant, with suggestions for various ways to repeat it. Sing or say the rhyme quickly and slowly, loudly and quietly, while bouncing, patting your lap, or clapping to keep a rhythm. Add movements and animal noises or snoring as desired, mimicking the action in the rhyme. Encourage the children's caregivers to adapt movements or make up new ones as appropriate for their child. Possible motions for babies and older children are included. Share one rhyme several times during a single storytime, and repeat the same rhyme over several storytimes.

Early Literacy Activities

These activities follow the seven focus areas recommended in Every Child Ready to Read @

Your Library, an early literacy partnership project between the Public Library Association and the Association for Library Service to Children, divisions of the American Library Association, and the National Institute of Child Health and Human Development (NICHD) of the National Institutes of Health (see www.pla.org/earlyliteracy.htm). A clear overview of these focus areas as well as innovative activity suggestions are included in *Early Literacy Storytimes @ Your Library* by Saroj Nadkarni Ghoting and Pamela Martin-Diaz (American Library Assn., 2006).

Consider integrating several (not all) of the Early Literacy Activities or techniques suggested below as you share the nursery rhyme. All activities should be approached in a fun and playful manner, encouraging curiosity and allowing for children's individual differences. Avoid any tendencies toward drill or rote memorization (Yopp 702). **Note:** Be aware of children's developmental stages and focus on the activities that are appropriate to the ages and stages of your group. The suggestions provided are intended to give you a variety of ideas to work with over time. You will not incorporate all of the techniques into any one rhyme, or even all into one storytime. Try different activities to highlight a different skill during each storytime.

Print Motivation

- Encourage interest in and excitement about reading and books. Say the words rhythmically and with enthusiasm.

- Create voices for the characters, and change your tone and facial expression as appropriate to the context to convey your enjoyment of the rhyme.

- Repeat the rhyme several times together with the children, encouraging their own enjoyment and internalization of its lively rhythms.

Language and Vocabulary

- Introduce and explain new words or new meanings to familiar words. Use the rhyme pieces to illustrate, pointing to the pictures of the words you are saying or the events you are describing.

- Talk or sing about the illustrations: "I see a haystack." "I see a cow." Pause for the children to name the object to which you are pointing: "I see a _____." Expand on descriptive features of the illustrations to build vocabulary and encourage the children's awareness of and attention to details. For example: "I see a boy. A boy wearing a blue hat and blue clothes."

Phonological Awareness

- Play with rhymes, practice breaking words apart and putting them back together, and listen for beginning sounds and alliteration. Play with the words, objects, and names in the rhyme and change them (see each chapter for examples). Use puppets or props to dramatize the alternate word choices.

- Explain that rhyming words sound the same at the end, and give examples. Try pausing just before the end of a rhyming pair and encourage the children to supply the rhyming word with the support of visual clues or context, or simply through the sounds suggested by the rhyme.

- Play an "oddity task" game. For example, which word does not rhyme? Horn, sheep, corn. *(Answer: sheep.)* Which word sounds different at the beginning? Diddle, fiddle, dog. *(Answer: fiddle.)* Which word sounds different at the end? Cat, hat, dog. *(Answer: dog.)*

- Blend word parts in a variety of ways.

  Syllables: dump … ling. What's the word? *(Dumpling.)*

  Onset sound: /d/ … og. What's the word? *(Dog.)* What other words start with /d/? (Note that the symbol / / signifies the sound of the letter.)

  Phoneme by phoneme (for older children, in primary grades): /m/-/oo/-/n/. What's the word? *(Moon.)*

- Practice segmenting or "stretching" the nursery rhyme words (for older children, in primary grades). Show the children a rubber band and stretch it out and in. As you stretch the rubber band out longer, you can see all of its parts more clearly. Explain that you can also stretch words, so that you can hear each individual sound (phoneme) in the word. Stretch the word "on": /o/-/n/. Sometimes one phoneme is represented by more than one letter, such as in the name "John": /J/-/oh/-/n/. "John" contains three phonemes. Stretch other nursery rhyme words.

- Clap words: Clap once for each word in the rhyme, following the poster. Introduce variety by stomping feet or jumping once for each word.

- Clap syllables: Slightly older children can learn to clap once for each syllable in the rhyme. Practice with one word at a time as the children begin to understand the concept. For example: Did-dle (2 claps); Diddle (2 claps); Dump-ling (2 claps); my (1 clap); son (1 clap); John (1 clap). Introduce variety by stomping feet or jumping to the syllables.

- Sing the nursery rhyme to its familiar tune. Follow the musical notations and autoharp/guitar chords provided if desired.

Print Awareness

- Help the children notice print, know how to handle books, and follow the written word on a page. Point to the poster included in the companion kit and say: "Our nursery rhyme is written right up here. I'll read it aloud, and then we'll say it again together." Follow the text of the rhyme with your finger as you read the poster, from left to right to reinforce print directionality as well as the concept that print stands for spoken language.

- Occasionally turn the poster upside down or sideways and see if the children detect the problem.

Narrative Skills

- Practice retelling stories or events with the children, sequencing the order in which events happened, and adding descriptions. Talk and ask open-ended questions about

the rhyme and the objects and characters in it, and allow the children to ask questions. Avoid asking yes/no questions unless there is a specific purpose in doing so. Qualify questions by including the phrase, "do you think," such as in "Why do you think ...?" or "What do you think ...?" This type of question does not have a "right" answer that children are afraid they will get wrong. Talk about ways in which we may have experiences or feelings that are similar to those of the nursery rhyme characters. For example, how do you think Little Boy Blue will feel when he wakes up and finds that the sheep are in the meadow and the cows are eating the corn?

- If you have a small enough group and adequate time, act out the rhyme with creative dramatics. Make sure each child gets to play all of the roles if possible, and to choose who or what they want to be.

- Consider incorporating craft activities into the program as a springboard for the children to retell rhymes and stories. (See "Take-home Rhyme Pieces" and "Additional Extension Ideas" in each chapter.)

- As the children's repertoire of nursery rhyme friends grows, ask "Who am I?" nursery rhyme riddles. For example: "I blow my horn to call the sheep and the cows. I fell asleep under a haystack. Who am I?" (*Answer: Little Boy Blue.*)

Letter Knowledge

- Help the children learn to recognize and identify letters; to know that they have different names and sounds; and to understand that the same letter can look different. Begin with letter sounds that young children can articulate easily, and introduce the sounds in the general order they develop in children's speech. (See www.pla.org/ala/pla/plaissues/earlylit/workshops parent/lettersounds.pdf.)

Choose word examples that correspond to the letter sounds. For example, "S is for Sock." Avoid word examples such as "S is for

Sheep," which begins with the "sh" sound rather than a hard "s."

Introduce this group of letters first, one at a time, though not necessarily in this order:

    B, M, D, T, W, P, N, Y, H

Introduce this group of letters next:

    S, F, G, V, Z, K, C

Introduce this group of letters last:

    L, R, J

Parent/Caregiver Connection

- Reinforce the parent/caregiver's key role in their child's early literacy development through comfortable, relaxed times together with songs, rhymes, and books.

- Encourage parents/caregivers to participate during storytime and to incorporate nursery rhymes at home during play and reading times. Select one of the early literacy activities that you share together during storytime, and briefly explain how the activity supports children's early literacy development. Suggest repeating the activity at home. Try different activities to highlight different skills during each storytime.

- Share information about Dialogic, or "Hear and Say" Reading (see Resources). Encourage parents and caregivers to individually discuss the day's rhyme, its characters, and events in an open-ended way with their children, following the child's interest while affirming and expanding upon their answers. Build on the things that catch the child's interest. This type of positive, interactive discussion around familiar rhymes and books helps improve early language development, communication, and parent/child relationships.

- Share brief facts about the direct benefits of reading to children and of playing word games with them.

- Model enthusiastic reading behaviors and interactions, emphasizing fun and enjoyment as the goals.

Take-home Rhyme Pieces

- Distribute take-home card stock illustrations of the day's nursery rhyme (included in each rhyme chapter), and either color and assemble them at the end of storytime or encourage the families to do so at home. Make a sample of the take-home version, and demonstrate singing or saying the rhyme using the small-size piece(s). (Families may affix sticky-back magnet material to pieces for playtime use on a magnetic surface such as a cookie sheet or the refrigerator if desired. Be aware of choking hazard considerations for younger children.)

Additional Extension Ideas

- Make companion crafts for the day's nursery rhyme, providing materials for both children and adults, or share storybooks extending the rhyme's theme, content, or concepts.

- Display nursery rhyme and children's poetry books and make them available for your audience to borrow and share at home. Emphasize that the books don't need to be read from cover to cover. Encourage children and their caregivers to take turns selecting poems and rhymes as they read, and to talk about details of illustrations that accompany the text. Show pictures from several different nursery rhyme books that illustrate the day's nursery rhyme, and repeat the rhyme together with each new illustration. Some classic and favorite Mother Goose books are listed in the bibliography.

- Build a nursery rhyme village, make a giant map of Mother Goose Town, orchestrate a Mother Goose Musical performance, or celebrate International Mother Goose Day (May 1).

- Let your creativity run wild, and have fun!

The ideas detailed in this volume, together with the nursery rhyme poster and character set from the companion kit, provide tools and techniques to help you successfully weave nursery rhymes and related activities into the fabric of your storytimes and curriculum. I hope that these methods will help you gain confidence and facility in sharing nursery rhymes, and also provide you with a deeper understanding of the enduring benefits afforded by actively sharing this rich tradition with your children, their families, and caregivers.

References

Nursery Rhymes and Early Literacy

Adams, Marilyn Jager. *Beginning to Read: Thinking and Learning About Print*. MIT Press, 1990.

Blevins, Wiley. *Phonemic Awareness Activities for Early Reading Success: Easy, Playful Activities That Prepare Children for Phonics Instruction*. Scholastic Professional Books, 1997.

Bryant, P. E., and L. Bradley, M. MacLean, J. Crossland. "Nursery Rhymes, Phonological Skills and Reading." *Journal of Child Language*, 16.2 (1989): 407–428.

Bryant, P. E., M. MacLean, L. L. Bradley, and J. Crossland. (1990). "Rhyme and Alliteration, Phoneme Detection, and Learning to Read." *Developmental Psychology*, 26.3 (1990): 429–438.

Fox, Mem. *Reading Magic: Why Reading Aloud to Our Children Will Change their Lives Forever*. Harcourt, 2001.

Geller, Linda Gibson. "Children's Rhymes and Literacy Learning: Making Connections." *Language Arts*, 60.2 (1983): 184–193.

Ghoting, Saroj Nadkarni, and Pamela Martin-Diaz. *Early Literacy Storytimes @ Your Library: Partnering with Caregivers for Success*. American Library Assn., 2006.

Hempenstall, Kerry. "The Role of Phonemic Awareness in Beginning Reading: A Review." *Behaviour Change*, 14 (1997): 201–214.

The International Reading Association and the National Association for the Education of Young Children. *Learning to Read and Write: Developmentally Appropriate Practices for Young Children*. www.naeyc.org/about/positions/pdf/PSREAD98.PDF. 1998.

Kirtley, Clare, Peter Bryant, Morag MacLean, and Lynette Bradley. "Rhyme, Rime, and the Onset of Reading." *Journal of Experimental Child Psychology*, 48 (1989): 224–245.

MacLean, Morag, Peter Bryant, and Lynette Bradley. "Rhymes, Nursery Rhymes, and Reading in Early Childhood." *Merrill-Palmer Quarterly*, 33.3 (1987): 255–281.

Morrow, Lesley Mandel. *Getting Ready to Read with Mother Goose*. Sadlier-Oxford, 2001.

Morrow, Lesley Mandel. *Literacy Development in the Early Years: Helping Children Read and Write*. 4th ed. Allyn & Bacon, 2001.

National Research Council. Catherine Snow, M. Susan Burns, and Peg Griffin, eds. *Preventing Reading Difficulties in Young Children*. National Academy Press, 1998.

Project ECLIPSE. "Mother Goose: A Scholarly Exploration." 31 Dec. 2005. www.eclipse.rutgers.edu/goose/literacy/.

Sadlier-Oxford. "Nursery Rhymes and Phonemic Awareness." Professional Development Series, Volume 3. Sadlier-Oxford, 2000.

Yopp, Hallie Kay. "Developing Phonemic Awareness in Young Children." *The Reading Teacher*, 45.9 (1992): 696–703.

Zero to Three. "Brain Wonders: Early Literacy." 31 Dec. 2005. www.zerotothree.org/brainwonders/EarlyLiteracy.html.

Here Am I

> Here am I,
>
> Little Jumping Joan.
>
> When nobody's with me,
>
> I'm all alone.

Variants

A few versions replace the last line with "I'm always alone."

History

Although possibly of bawdy origin with "Jumping Joan" as a questionable character, the rhyme has endured with few alterations. When chanted with young children, the rhythm of "Here Am I" offers a wonderful opportunity for enthusiastic jumping up and down!

Musical Notation

See rhythm notation on page 17.

Preparing and Using the Mother Goose Rhyme Time Pieces

"Here Am I" pieces:

• Jumping Joan girl

• "Here Am I" poster

Before sharing the rhyme, place the poster on an easel so the audience can see it clearly. Hold Jumping Joan in one or both hands. Actions for the rhyme are very simple, so you should be able to hold Jumping Joan throughout the rhyme and jump with her or bounce her on your lap.

Utilize the sections of Mother Goose Rhyme Time that work best for you and your storytime group or classroom. Experiment with new ideas and techniques. Practice ahead of time so you feel comfortable with the material and can focus on the audience rather than on trying to remember how you intended to share the rhyme.

Storytime

Share "Here Am I," rhythmically bouncing or jumping enthusiastically to keep a rhythm. Chant the rhyme quickly and slowly, loudly and quietly. This is a favorite!

Babies *(Sitting on caregivers' laps)*

> Here am I,
> *(Bounce baby or clap baby's feet rhythmically throughout.)*
> Little Jumping Joan.
> When nobody's with me,
> I'm all alone.

Older Children *(Standing)*

> Here am I,
> *(Jump rhythmically and enthusiastically throughout!)*
> Little Jumping Joan.
> When nobody's with me,
> I'm all alone.

Early Literacy Activities

Consider integrating one or several of the activities or techniques suggested below as you share the nursery rhyme. All activities should be approached in a fun and playful manner, encouraging curiosity and allowing for children's individual differences. **Note:** Be aware of children's developmental stages and focus on the activities that are appropriate for the ages and stages of your group. The suggestions provided are intended to give you a variety of ideas to work with over time. You will not incorporate all of the techniques at once. Share one rhyme several times during a single storytime, and repeat the same rhyme over several storytimes. Try different activities to highlight a different skill during each storytime.

Print Motivation (*Encourage interest in and excitement about reading and books.*)

- Say the words rhythmically and with enthusiasm, conveying your enjoyment of the rhyme.

- Repeat the rhyme several times together with the children, encouraging their own enjoyment and internalization of its lively rhythms.

Language and Vocabulary (*Introduce and explain new words or new meanings to familiar words.*)

- Use the rhyme pieces to illustrate and help explain language and vocabulary. Say: "This girl's name is Joan (*point to Joan*). She says 'Here am I,' which means 'Here I am.' 'Jumping Joan' must be her nickname, because she loves to jump! When nobody's with her, she is by herself, so she is all alone."

- Talk or sing about the illustrations: "I see a girl." "I see a shoe." Pause for the children to name the object to which you are pointing: "I see a _____." Expand on descriptive features of the illustrations to build vocabulary and encourage the children's awareness of and attention to details: "I see a girl. A girl with long hair who is jumping."

Phonological Awareness (*Play with rhymes, practice breaking words apart and putting them back together, and listen for beginning sounds and alliteration.*)

- Play with the words, situation, and names in the rhyme and change them. For example:

Here am I,
Little Jumping Joan.
When somebody's with me,
I'm not alone.

Here am I,
Little Jumping Jack.
My friends went away,
But they'll be right back!

- Explain that rhyming words sound the same at the end. "Joan" and "alone"; and "Jack" and "back" are rhyming word pairs. Try pausing just before the end of a rhyming pair and encourage the children to supply the rhyming word (such as "back" above) with the support of visual clues or context, or simply through the sounds suggested by the rhyme.

- Play an "oddity task" game. For example, which word does not rhyme? Joan, alone, here. (*Answer: here.*) Which word sounds different at the beginning? Jumping, with, Joan. (*Answer: with.*)

- Blend word parts in a variety of ways.

  <u>Syllables:</u> jump ... ing. What's the word? (*Jumping.*)

  <u>Onset sound:</u> /J/ ... oan. What's the word/name? (*Joan.*) What other words and names start with /j/?

  <u>Phoneme by phoneme (for older children, in primary grades):</u> /m/-/e/. What's the word? (*Me.*)

- Practice segmenting or "stretching" the nursery rhyme words (for older children, in primary grades). Show the children a rubber band and stretch it out and in. As you stretch the rubber band out longer, you can see all of its parts more clearly. Explain that you can also stretch words, so that you can hear each individual sound (phoneme) in the word. Stretch the word "me"; /m/-/e/. Sometimes one phoneme is represented by more than one letter, such as in the word "with": /w/-/i/-/th/. "With" contains three phonemes. Stretch other nursery rhyme words.

- Clap (or jump) words: Clap or jump once for each word in the rhyme, following the poster.

- Clap (or jump) syllables: Older children can learn to clap or jump once for each syllable in the rhyme. Practice with one word at a time as the children begin to understand the concept. For example: Here (1 clap); am (1 clap); I (1 clap); Lit-tle (2 claps); Jump-ing (2 claps); Joan (1 clap).

Print Awareness (*Notice print and know how to handle books and follow the written word on a page.*)

- Point to the "Here Am I" poster. Say: "Our nursery rhyme is written right up here. I'll read it aloud, and then we'll say it again together." Follow the text of the rhyme with your finger as you read the poster, from left to right.

- Occasionally turn the poster upside down or sideways and see if the children detect the problem.

Narrative Skills (*Practice retelling stories or events, sequencing the order in which events happened, and adding descriptions.*)

- Talk and ask two or three open-ended questions about the rhyme and the character and activity in it, and allow the children to ask questions. Avoid asking yes/no questions unless there is a specific purpose in doing so. Qualify questions by including the phrase "do you think," as in "Why do you think ...?" or "What do you think ...?" This type of question does not have a "right" answer that children are afraid they will get wrong. For example: Why do you think Joan is jumping so much? Why do you think she is all alone? Where do you think her friends might have gone? Do you think she has any brothers or sisters? What do you think Joan will do when she stops jumping?

- Change the name "Joan" to each of the children's names in turn as they take turns jumping to the rhyme.

Letter Knowledge—Letter H (*Learn to recognize and identify letters, knowing that they have different names and sounds and that the same letter can look different.*)

- Show a large size cutout or magnet-backed foam letter "H" and "h" (see Resources). Point to the capital "H" letter that begins the word "Here" in the title of your poster. Say. "Here is the letter H—a big uppercase, or capital H." Draw the capital letter "H" in the air as a group. Point to a small letter "h" on the poster within the rhyme's text. Say: "Here is also the letter h—a small, lowercase h." Draw a lowercase "h" in the air as a group. Make the breathy /H/ sound and say: "H is for Here; H is for Hello; H is for House; H is for Hand; H is for Help; H is for Horse; H is for Head; H is for Hat; H is for Hiccup; H is for Happy." Encourage the audience to repeat each phrase after you. Include three or four examples.

- Demonstrate making the shapes of "H" and "h" using string or pipe cleaners.

Parent/Caregiver Connection

- Reinforce the parent/caregiver's key role in their child's early literacy development through comfortable, relaxed times together with songs, rhymes, and books. Emphasize fun and enjoyment as the goals.

- Encourage caregivers to participate during storytime and to incorporate "Here Am I" at home during play and reading times. Select one of the "Here Am I" early literacy activities that you share together during storytime, and briefly explain how the activity supports children's early literacy development. Suggest repeating the activity at home. Try different activities to highlight different skills during each storytime.

- Share information about Dialogic, or "Hear and Say" Reading (see Resources). Encourage parents and caregivers to individually discuss the day's rhyme, its characters, and events in an open-ended way with their children, following the child's interest while affirming and expanding upon their answers. For example, point to Joan in "Here Am I" and ask, "Who is this?" Child: "A girl." Follow up with positive affirmation, and enlarge: "Yes, it's a girl named Joan. What is she doing?" Child:

"Jumping." Expand: "Yes, the girl is jumping up and down." Help the child repeat longer phrases. Ask open-ended questions such as: "What do you see in this picture?" Build on the things that catch the child's interest. This type of positive, interactive discussion around familiar rhymes and books helps improve early language development, communication, and parent/child relationships.

Take-home "Here Am I"

Copy the "Here Am I" illustration from page 18 onto card stock and distribute. Color and cut out the pieces at the end of storytime, or encourage the families to do so at home. Make a sample of the take-home version, and demonstrate chanting the rhyme using the small pieces. (Families may affix sticky-back magnet material to pieces for playtime use on a magnetic surface such as a cookie sheet or the refrigerator if desired. Be aware of choking hazard considerations for younger children.)

Additional Extension Ideas

Note: For all craft activities, provide materials for adult attendees as well as children. Encourage children and adults to talk together about what they are making, and to use the completed crafts to retell or act out the rhyme.

- Show the pictures from several different nursery rhyme books that illustrate "Here Am I" and repeat the rhyme together with each new illustration. Talk about the differences between the various illustrations.

- Have each child jump a specified number of times. Count the number of jumps aloud as a group.

- Pretend that Little Jumping Joan in the rhyme is an animal, and jump accordingly. For example, if Joan is a little kangaroo, how would she jump? How about if she is a baby elephant? How about a mouse?

- Use a Dancing Jack folk rhythm instrument to keep the beat as you say the rhyme. Allow the children to take turns holding the doll as you tap the board, or vice versa.

- Make a "Jumping Joan" pantin puppet. Cut out a head and body piece together, two separate arms, two thighs, and two calves with feet from card stock. Attach the body pieces at the shoulders, hips, and knees with metal brad paper fasteners or knotted yarn. Tie a string to the top of each arm, going across horizontally between the arms; and tie another string to the top of each leg, going across horizontally between the legs. Connect these two pieces of string to a third vertical piece of string, leaving a strand of it dangling below the puppet. Tie a separate piece of string to the top of the puppet's head. Hold the top string and pull the string below to make the pantin puppet "jump." See *Toys and Tales from Grandmother's Attic* by Edie Kraska (Houghton Mifflin, 1979) for detailed instructions if necessary.

- Make the shapes of "H" and "h" using string, pipe cleaners, or clay.

Here Am I

Chanted

Here am I,

Lit - tle Jump-ing Joan. When

no — bod-y's with me, I'm all a — lone.

Take-home Here Am I

Here am I,

Little Jumping Joan.

When nobody's with me,

I'm all alone.

Little Bo-Peep

> Little Bo-Peep has lost her sheep,
>
> And doesn't know where to find them.
>
> Leave them alone, and they'll come home,
>
> Wagging their tails behind them.

Variants

In some versions the sheep come home "Bringing their tails behind them."

Additional verses first appearing in 1810 are:

Verse 2
Little Bo-Peep fell fast asleep,
And dreamed she heard them bleating;
But when she awoke, she found it a joke,
For they were still a-fleeting.

Verse 3
Then up she took her little crook,
Determined for to find them;
She found them indeed, but it made
    her heart bleed,
For they'd left all their tails behind them.

Verse 4
It happened one day, as Bo-Peep did stray
Into a meadow hard by,
There she espied their tails side by side,
All hung on a tree to dry.

Verse 5
She heaved a sigh, and wiped her eye,
And over the hillocks went rambling/
stump-o;
She tried what she could, as a shepherdess
    should,
To tack each again to its lambkin/rump-o.

History

First recorded in 1810, "Little Bo-Peep" has gained enormous popularity and is routinely included in modern nursery rhyme volumes. The rhyme possibly began as an accompaniment to the baby game of "peek-a-boo" or "boe-pepe," which has been traced to the sixteenth century. Opie notes that despite the rhyme's later documented date, it was almost certainly known in the eighteenth century as evidenced by its similarity to some pieces popular in the 1760s. For example, a version of the song "Yankee Doodle" (printed circa 1777) includes: "Our Jemima's lost her Mare / And can't tell where to find her, / But she'll come trotting by and by / And bring her Tail behind her."

"Little Bo-Peep's" several references to the lambs' tails likely refer to the practice of bringing lambs in from the pasture to have their tails bobbed.

Musical Notation

See musical notation on page 25.

Preparing and Using the Mother Goose Rhyme Time Pieces

"Little Bo-Peep" pieces:

- Little Bo-Peep shepherdess girl

- Group of sheep in a row; end sheep with movable tail

- "Little Bo-Peep" poster

Partially hide the group of sheep nearby before the audience arrives, so that a portion of them is visible. Before sharing the rhyme, place the poster on an easel so the audience can see it clearly.

Hold up Little Bo-Peep in one hand as you begin the rhyme. Help her search around for her sheep, one hand above your eyes, then affix her to a large Velcro or magnet board so your hands are free to produce the sheep and make the end sheep's tail wag back and forth. If you wish to incorporate group motions or use a musical instrument for accompaniment, leave Little Bo-Peep up on the board while you lead the group in the actions or play and sing the song. Hide the group of sheep behind the board so that you can produce them again and again as they "come home."

Utilize the sections of Mother Goose Rhyme Time that work best for you and your storytime group or classroom. Experiment with new ideas and techniques. Practice ahead of time so you feel comfortable with the material and can focus on the audience rather than on trying to remember how you intended to share the rhyme.

Storytime

Share "Little Bo-Peep" as a song or as a chant; bouncing, patting your lap, or clapping to keep a rhythm. Sing or say the rhyme quickly and slowly, loudly and quietly. Add movements and animal noises as desired. Encourage the children's caregivers to adapt motions or make up new ones as appropriate for their child; many different actions are possible. Here are a few options:

Babies (*Sitting on caregivers' laps*)

Little Bo-Peep has lost her sheep,
(*Rock baby rhythmically throughout.*)
And doesn't know where to find them.
Leave them alone, and they'll come home,
Wagging their tails behind them.

Older Children (*Standing*)

Little Bo-Peep has lost her sheep,
(*Hand over eyes as if searching.*)
And doesn't know where to find them.
(*Hands out questioningly.*)
Leave them alone, and they'll come home,
(*Nod head.*)
Wagging their tails behind them.
(*Wag behinds, "baaa."*)

Early Literacy Activities

Consider integrating one or several of the activities or techniques suggested below as you share the nursery rhyme. All activities should be approached in a fun and playful manner, encouraging curiosity and allowing for children's individual differences. **Note:** Be aware of children's developmental stages and focus on the activities that are appropriate for the ages and stages of your group. The suggestions provided are intended to give you a variety of ideas to work with over time. You will not incorporate all of the techniques at once. Share one rhyme several times during a single storytime, and repeat the same rhyme over several storytimes. Try different activities to highlight a different skill during each storytime.

Print Motivation (*Encourage interest in and excitement about reading and books.*)

- Say the words rhythmically and with enthusiasm, conveying your enjoyment of the rhyme.

- Repeat the rhyme several times together with the children, encouraging their own enjoyment and internalization of its gentle rhythms.

Language and Vocabulary (*Introduce and explain new words or new meanings to familiar words.*)

- Use the rhyme pieces to illustrate and help explain language and vocabulary. Say: "This girl is named Little Bo-Peep (*point to girl*). She is a shepherdess, which means she takes care of a flock, or a group, of sheep. If she was a boy, she would be called a shepherd. Little Bo-Peep is holding a curved stick or staff in her hand. It is called a "shepherd's crook." In our rhyme, Little Bo-Peep's sheep are lost! We are telling her that the sheep will find their way home by themselves."

- Talk or sing about the illustrations: "I see a girl." "I see a sheep." Pause for the children to name the object to which you are pointing: "I see a _____." Expand on descriptive features of the illustrations to build vocabulary and encourage the children's awareness of and attention to details: "I see a girl. A girl wearing a blue bonnet and a white apron."

Phonological Awareness *(Play with rhymes, practice breaking words apart and putting them back together, and listen for beginning sounds and alliteration.)*

- Play with Little Bo-Peep's name and the animals in the rhyme and change them. Use puppets or props to dramatize. For example:

  Little Bo-Pow has lost her *cow.*
  Little Bo-Pat has lost her *cat.*
  Little Bo-Pog has lost her *dog.*

- Explain that rhyming words sound the same at the end. "Pow" and "cow" rhyme, as do "pat" and "cat"; and "pog" and "dog." Try pausing just before the end of a rhyming pair and encourage the children to supply the rhyming word (such as "cow" and "cat" and "dog" above) with the support of visual clues or context, or simply through the sounds suggested by the rhyme.

- Play an "oddity task" game. For example, which word does not rhyme? Peep, lost, sheep. *(Answer: lost.)* Which word sounds different at the beginning? Her, home, come. *(Answer: come.)* Which word sounds different at the end? Them, lost, doesn't. *(Answer: them.)*

- Blend word parts in a variety of ways.

  <u>Syllables:</u> lit ... tle. What's the word? *(Little.)*

  <u>Onset sound:</u> /l/ ... ost. What's the word? *(Lost.)* What other words start with /l/?

  <u>Phoneme by phoneme (for older children, in primary grades):</u> /f/-/i/-/n/-/d/. What's the word? *(Find.)*

- Practice segmenting or "stretching" the nursery rhyme words (for older children, in primary grades). Show the children a rubber band and stretch it out and in. As you stretch the rubber band out longer, you can see all of its parts more clearly. Explain that you can also stretch words, so that you can hear each individual sound (phoneme) in the word. Stretch the word "lost": /l/-/o/-/s/-/t/. Sometimes one phoneme is represented by more than one letter, such as in the word "sheep": /sh/-/ee/-/p/. "Sheep" contains three phonemes. Stretch other nursery rhyme words.

- Clap words: Clap once for each word in the rhyme, following the poster. Introduce variety by stomping feet or jumping once for each word.

- Clap syllables: Older children can learn to clap once for each syllable in the rhyme. Practice with one word at a time as the children begin to understand the concept. For example: Lit-tle (2 claps); Bo-Peep (2 claps); has (1 clap); lost (1 clap); her (1 clap); sheep (1 clap). Introduce variety by stomping feet or jumping to the syllables.

Print Awareness *(Notice print and know how to handle books and follow the written word on a page.)*

- Point to the "Little Bo-Peep" poster. Say: "Our nursery rhyme is written right up here. I'll read it aloud, and then we'll say it again together." Follow the text of the rhyme with your finger as you read the poster, from left to right.

- Occasionally turn the poster upside down or sideways and see if the children detect the problem.

Narrative Skills *(Practice retelling stories or events, sequencing the order in which events happened, and adding descriptions.)*

- Talk and ask two or three open-ended questions about the rhyme and the objects and characters in it, and allow the children to ask questions. Avoid asking yes/no questions unless there is a specific purpose in doing so. Qualify questions by including the phrase "do you think," as in "Why do you think ...?" or "What do you think ...?" This type of question does not have a "right" answer that children are afraid they will get wrong. For example: How do you think Little Bo-Peep's sheep became lost? What do you think Little Bo-Peep was doing when the sheep became lost? Where do you think the sheep might have gone? How do you think Little Bo-Peep felt when her sheep were lost? How do think she felt when the lost sheep came home again? Why do you think the sheep were wagging their tails when they came home?

- If you have a small enough group and adequate time, act out "Little Bo-Peep" with creative dramatics. Have several children at a time be shepherdesses or shepherds (change the rhyme to "her sheep" or "his sheep," accordingly), searching in vain for their sheep. The other children are the sheep, hiding from Little Bo-Peep until the last line of the rhyme when they run out and follow her or him. Make sure that each child gets to play both roles if desired.

Letter Knowledge—Letter B (*Learn to recognize and identify letters, knowing that they have different names and sounds and that the same letter can look different.*)

- Show a large-size cutout or magnet-backed foam letter "B" and "b" (see Resources). Point to the capital "B" letter that begins the name "Bo-Peep" in the title of your poster. Say: "Here is the letter B—a big uppercase, or capital B." Draw the capital letter "B" in the air as a group. Point to a small letter "b" on the poster within the rhyme's text. Say: "Here is also the letter b—a small, lower-case b." Draw a lowercase "b" in the air as a group. Make the /B/ sound and say: "B is for Bo-Peep; B is for Baby; B is for Boy; B is for Bed; B is for Ball; B is for Bike; B is for Bear; B is for Balloon; B is for Book." Encourage the audience to repeat each phrase after you. Include three or four examples.

- Demonstrate making the shapes of "B" and "b" using string or pipe cleaners.

Parent/Caregiver Connection

- Reinforce the parent/caregiver's key role in their child's early literacy development through comfortable, relaxed times together with songs, rhymes, and books. Emphasize fun and enjoyment as the goals.

- Encourage caregivers to participate during storytime and to incorporate "Little Bo-Peep" at home during play and reading times. Select one of the "Little Bo-Peep" early literacy activities that you share together during storytime, and briefly explain how the activity supports children's early literacy development. Suggest repeating the activity at home. Try different activities to highlight different skills during each storytime.

- Share information about Dialogic, or "Hear and Say" Reading (see Resources). Encourage parents and caregivers to individually discuss the day's rhyme, its characters, and events in an open-ended way with their children, following the child's interest while affirming and expanding upon their answers. For example, point to Little Bo-Peep in "Little Bo-Peep" and ask, "Who is this?" Child: "A girl." Follow up with positive affirmation, and enlarge: "Yes, it's a girl named Little Bo-Peep. What do you notice about Little Bo-Peep?" Child: "She's looking." Expand: "Yes, Little Bo-Peep seems to be looking for something, holding her hand over her eyes." Help the child repeat longer phrases. Ask open-ended questions such as: "What do you see in this picture?" Build on the things that catch the child's interest. This type of positive, interactive discussion around familiar rhymes and books helps improve early language development, communication, and parent/child relationships.

Take-home "Little Bo-Peep"

Copy the "Little Bo-Peep" illustrations from pages 26–27 onto card stock and distribute. Color, cut out, and assemble the pieces at the end of storytime, or encourage the families to do so at home. Attach the sheep tail at the dot with a metal brad fastener or with knotted yarn.

Make a sample of the take-home version, and demonstrate singing or saying the rhyme using the small pieces. (Families may affix sticky-back magnet material to pieces for playtime use on a magnetic surface such as a cookie sheet or the refrigerator if desired. Be aware of choking hazard considerations for younger children.)

Additional Extension Ideas

Note: For all craft activities, provide materials for adult attendees as well as children. Encourage children and adults to talk together about what they are making, and to use the completed crafts to retell or act out the rhyme.

- Show the pictures from several different nursery rhyme books that illustrate "Little Bo-Peep" and repeat the rhyme together with each new illustration. Talk about the differences between the various illustrations.

- Make paper plate sheep with wagging tails! Cut out sheep faces with ears, four legs, and tails from card stock or construction paper. Glue the faces and legs onto the paper plate sheep body, and affix the tail with a metal brad fastener or with knotted yarn. Wag the sheep tails back and forth as you say "Little Bo-Peep."

- Talk about: Long ago, there were no sheep farms. A shepherd or shepherdess took care of the sheep for several families, wandering around the countryside with the sheep and protecting them as they ate grass in the meadows. Being a shepherd or shepherdess was a very lonely job!

- Talk about: How would you be able to gather a whole lot of sheep together? They don't come when you call! Sheep dogs are especially trained to help take care of a flock of sheep. "Herding dogs" chase sheep together into a group by running around them, and then push and guide the flock in certain directions. A shepherd communicates with the dogs through different whistled signals that tell the dogs what to do and where the shepherd wants the sheep to go. The dogs are quiet while herding the sheep, because barking would make the sheep become scared and wild. Some herding dogs are also "guard dogs" that stay in the pasture with the flock and protect them from wolves, coyotes, and other wild animals. Sometimes shepherds use donkeys or llamas instead of dogs to guard their sheep! Donkeys and llamas are natural enemies of wolves and coyotes, and chase the predators away if they come near the sheep!

- Hide enough cutout paper sheep around the room so that each child in your group can find one for a "lost sheep hunt." When each child finds one of the sheep, have him or her return to the story area with the sheep. When all of the children have found a sheep, have them bring them up to a "sheep pen" box one at a time as you count them together.

- Read *Mary Had A Little Lamb* by Sarah Josepha Hale. Several versions of note are a contemporary interpretation photo illustrated by Bruce McMillan (Scholastic, 1990); an expanded version showing what happens after the lamb gets to school, adapted by Mary Ann Hoberman (Little, Brown and Company, 2003); and a tale describing what happens when the lamb decides to go off alone told and illustrated by Iza Trapani (Whispering Coyote Press, 1998).

- Read *Sheep Take a Hike* by Nancy Shaw, illustrated by Margot Apple (Houghton Mifflin, 1994). The sheep become lost during a chaotic hike in the great outdoors, but manage to find their way back by following the trail of wool they have left behind. See other adventures by the same group of indomitable sheep in *Sheep in a Jeep* (Houghton Mifflin, 1986); *Sheep on a Ship* (Houghton Mifflin, 1989); *Sheep in a Shop* (Houghton Mifflin, 1991); and *Sheep Out to Eat* (Houghton Mifflin, 1992).

- Make a Find Bo-Peep's Sheep Wheel craft. Complete instructions are included in the book *Crafts from your Favorite Children's Songs* by Kathy Ross (Millbrook Press, 2001).

- Make Sheep Paper Bag Puppets. Ask each child's sheep puppet whether it was truly lost, where it went, and so forth. Have the children hide their sheep puppets in the

room and call for them. See *A Pocketful of Puppets: Mother Goose* by Tamara Hunt and Nancy Renfro (Nancy Renfro Studios, 1998).

- Make a Little Bo-Peep Sleeve Puppet. Complete instructions are included in the book *Crafts From Your Favorite Nursery Rhymes* by Kathy Ross (Millbrook Press, 2002).

- Make Little Bo-Peep's Blue Ribbon Bonnet. Instructions are included in the book *What Can You Do with a Paper Bag?* by Judith Cressy (Chronicle Books, 2001).

- Share "Little Boy Blue and Little Bo-Peep" "in two voices" from *You Read to Me, I'll Read to You: Very Short Mother Goose Tales to Read Together* by Mary Ann Hoberman; illustrated by Michael Emberley (Little, Brown and Company, 2005). Before you begin, familiarize the children with the standard version of "Little Boy Blue" from a classic Mother Goose rhyme book or from *Mother Goose Rhyme Time: Night*.

- Make the shapes of "B" and "b" using string, pipe cleaners, or clay.

Little Bo-Peep

Melancholy

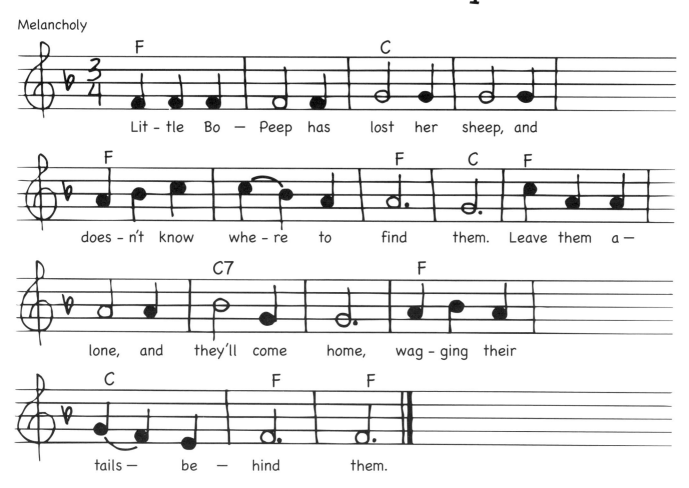

Lit - tle Bo — Peep has lost her sheep, and does - n't know whe - re to find them. Leave them a — lone, and they'll come home, wag - ging their tails — be — hind them.

Take-home Little Bo-Peep

Little Bo-Peep has lost her sheep,
And doesn't know where to find them.
Leave them alone, and they'll come home,
Wagging their tails behind them.

sheep tail

Little Jack Horner

> Little Jack Horner
>
> Sat in a corner,
>
> Eating a great big pie.
>
> He stuck in his thumb,
>
> And pulled out a plum,
>
> And said, "What a good child am I!"

Variants

Common versions of "Little Jack Horner" have him eating a "Christmas" pie, putting his thumb into the pie instead of sticking it in, and announcing "What a good boy am I!"

History

"Jack" Horner may have been Thomas Horner, steward to the abbot of Glastonbury, Richard Whiting. In an effort to ingratiate himself to the court, Whiting had the title deeds for 12 large Glastonbury estates baked into a pie as a Christmas gift for King Henry VIII (1491–1547). Hiding valuables inside of pastries was one medieval method of deceiving highwaymen and thieves. Tasked with delivering the offering, Horner supposedly stuck his thumb into the pie en route and withdrew one of the "plum" deeds for himself. The current owners of Mells Manor can indeed trace their lineage back to Thomas Horner, although they assert that their ancestor procured the estate in a more respectable fashion than is suggested by the rhyme.

Musical Notation

See musical notation on page 34.

Preparing and Using the Mother Goose Rhyme Time Pieces

"Little Jack Horner" pieces:

- Large pie with pie crust pocket and sitting boy with movable arm

- "Little Jack Horner" poster

Make sure that Jack's thumb with its plum is tucked down inside the pie crust pocket before the audience arrives. Hide the rhyme piece out of sight.

Before sharing the rhyme, place the poster on an easel so the audience can see it clearly. Hold Jack in one hand as you sing or say the rhyme. With your other hand, swivel his arm upward to produce the plum as you say "pulled out a plum." Motions for the rhyme are very simple, so you should be able to hold Jack through-out the rhyme while leading the group in the actions. If you wish to have your hands free to accompany yourself with a musical instrument, affix Jack to a large Velcro or magnet board. Make sure that you still manipulate his arm to produce the plum on cue!

Utilize the sections of Mother Goose Rhyme Time that work best for you and your storytime group or classroom. Experiment with new ideas and techniques. Practice ahead of time so you feel comfortable with the material and can focus on the audience rather than on trying to remember how you intended to share the rhyme.

Storytime

Share "Little Jack Horner" as a song or as a chant; bouncing, patting your lap, or clapping to keep a rhythm. Sing or say the rhyme quickly and slowly, loudly and quietly. Add movements and eating noises as desired. Encourage the children's caregivers to adapt motions or make up new ones as appropriate for their child; many different actions are possible. Here are a few options:

Babies (*Sitting on caregivers' laps*)

> Little Jack Horner
> (*Rock baby.*)
> Sat in a corner,
> Eating a great big pie.
> (*Make noisy eating sounds.*)
> He stuck in his thumb,
> (*Stick thumb downward into imaginary pie.*)
> And pulled out a plum,
> (*Point thumb upward.*)
> And said, "What a good child am I!"
> (*Hug baby.*)

Older Children (*Standing or sitting*)

> Little Jack Horner
> (*Rock or sway back and forth.*)
> Sat in a corner,
> Eating a great big pie.
> (*Pretend to eat noisily; arms out to show "big."*)
> He stuck in his thumb,
> (*Stick thumb downward into imaginary pie.*)
> And pulled out a plum,
> (*Point thumb upward.*)
> And said, "What a good child am I!"
> (*Nod head; point to self.*)

Early Literacy Activities

Consider integrating one or several of the activities or techniques suggested below as you share the nursery rhyme. All activities should be approached in a fun and playful manner, encouraging curiosity and allowing for chil-

dren's individual differences. **Note:** Be aware of children's developmental stages and focus on the activities that are appropriate for the ages and stages of your group. The suggestions provided are intended to give you a variety of ideas to work with over time. You will not incorporate all of the techniques at once. Share one rhyme several times during a single storytime, and repeat the same rhyme over several storytimes. Try different activities to highlight a different skill during each storytime.

Print Motivation (*Encourage interest in and excitement about reading and books.*)

- Say the words rhythmically and with enthusiasm, conveying your enjoyment of the rhyme.

- Create a voice for Jack, and change your tone and facial expression as appropriate to the context.

- Repeat the rhyme several times together with the children, encouraging their own enjoyment and internalization of its lively rhythms.

Language and Vocabulary (*Introduce and explain new words or new meanings to familiar words.*)

- Use the rhyme pieces to illustrate and help explain language and vocabulary. "This boy's name is Jack Horner (*point to Jack*). His first name is Jack, and his last name is Horner. He sat in a corner of the room, like one of our room's corners (*point to the corners of the room*) eating a really big pie (*point to pie illustration*). He stuck or put his thumb (*hold up your thumb*) into the pie. When he pulled out his thumb, there was a plum (*swivel Jack's thumb out of the pie and point to the plum*) sticking to it! A plum is a type of fruit (*show the children a real plum*)."

- Talk or sing about the illustrations: "I see a pie." "I see a plum." Pause for the children to name the object to which you are pointing: "I see a _____." Expand on descriptive features of the illustrations to build vocabulary and encourage the children's awareness of and attention to details: "I see a boy. A boy wearing a vest and holding a large pie on his lap."

Phonological Awareness (*Play with rhymes, practice breaking words apart and putting them back together, and listen for beginning sounds and alliteration.*)

- Explain that rhyming words sound the same at the end. Play an "oddity task" game. For example, which word does not rhyme? Horner, corner, eating. (*Answer: eating.*) Which word sounds different at the beginning? Great, pulled, plum. (*Answer: great.*) Which word sounds different at the end? Big, sat, out. (*Answer: big.*)

- Blend word parts in a variety of ways.

    Syllables: cor … ner. What's the word? (*Corner.*)

    Onset sound: /s/ … aid. What's the word? (*Said.*) What other words start with /s/?

    Phoneme by phoneme (for older children, in primary grades): /s/-/a/-/t/. What's the word? (*Sat.*)

- Practice segmenting or "stretching" the nursery rhyme words (for older children, in primary grades). Show the children a rubber band and stretch it out and in. As you stretch the rubber band out longer, you can see all of its parts more clearly. Explain that you can also stretch words, so that you can hear each individual sound (phoneme) in the word. Stretch the word "sat": /s/-/a/-/t/. Sometimes one phoneme is represented by more than one letter, such as in the name "Jack": /J/-/a/-/ck/. It contains three phonemes. Stretch other nursery rhyme words.

- Clap words: Clap once for each word in the rhyme, following the poster. Introduce variety by stomping feet or jumping once for each word.

- Clap syllables: Older children can learn to clap once for each syllable in the rhyme. Practice with one word at a time as the children begin to understand the concept. For example: Lit-tle (2 claps); Jack (1 clap); Hor-ner (2 claps); Sat (1 clap); in (1 clap); a (1 clap); cor-ner (2 claps). Introduce variety by stomping feet or jumping to the syllables.

Print Awareness (*Notice print and know how to handle books and follow the written word on a page.*)

- Point to the "Little Jack Horner" poster. Say: "Our nursery rhyme is written right up here. I'll read it aloud, and then we'll say it again together." Follow the text of the rhyme with your finger as you read the poster, from left to right.

- Occasionally turn the poster upside down or sideways and see if the children detect the problem.

Narrative Skills (*Practice retelling stories or events, sequencing the order in which events happened, and adding descriptions.*)

- Talk and ask two or three open-ended questions about the rhyme and the objects and characters in it, and allow the children to ask questions. Avoid asking yes/no questions unless there is a specific purpose in doing so. Qualify questions by including the phrase "do you think," as in "Why do you think …?" or "What do you think …?" This type of question does not have a "right" answer that children are afraid they will get wrong. For example: Why do you think Little Jack Horner is sitting in a corner? Do you think Jack is having a good time? If yes, why do you think so? Do you think there are other children around, or not? Do you think Jack will eat the whole pie all by himself? With whom might he share it? What do you think Jack will do when he's done with the pie?

- If you have a small enough group and adequate time, act out "Little Jack Horner" with creative dramatics using your Little Jack Horner's Pie crafts (see Additional Extension Ideas on page 32). Pull out various items one at a time, while singing or saying the rhyme as a group.

Letter Knowledge—Letter J (*Learn to recognize and identify letters, knowing that they have different names and sounds and that the same letter can look different.*)

- Show a large-size cutout or magnet-backed foam letter "J" and "j" (see Resources). Point to the capital "J" letter that begins the name "Jack" in the title of your poster. Say: "Here is the letter J—a big uppercase, or capital J." Draw the capital letter "J" in

the air as a group. Point to a small letter "j" on the poster within the rhyme's text. Say: "Here is also the letter j—a small, lowercase j." Draw a lowercase "j" in the air as a group. Make the /J/ sound and say: "J is for Jack; J is for Jump; J is for Jello; J is for Jam; J is for Juice." Encourage the audience to repeat each phrase after you. Include three or four examples.

- Demonstrate making the shapes of "J" and "j" using string or pipe cleaners.

Parent/Caregiver Connection

- Reinforce the parent/caregiver's key role in their child's early literacy development through comfortable, relaxed times together with songs, rhymes, and books. Emphasize fun and enjoyment as the goals.

- Encourage caregivers to participate during storytime and incorporate "Little Jack Horner" at home during play and reading times. Select one of the "Little Jack Horner" early literacy activities that you share together during storytime, and briefly explain how the activity supports children's early literacy development. Suggest repeating the activity at home. Try different activities to highlight different skills during each storytime.

- Share information about Dialogic, or "Hear and Say" Reading (see Resources). Encourage parents and caregivers to individually discuss the day's rhyme, its characters, and events in an open-ended way with their children, following the child's interest while affirming and expanding upon their answers. For example, point to Jack in "Little Jack Horner" and ask, "Who is this?" Child: "A boy." Follow up with positive affirmation, and enlarge: "Yes, it's a boy named Jack. What is he doing?" Child: "Pie." Expand: "Yes, he is eating a big pie." Help the child repeat longer phrases. Ask open-ended questions such as: "What do you see in this picture?" Build on the things that catch the child's interest. This type of positive, interactive discussion around familiar rhymes and books helps improve early language development, communication, and parent/child relationships.

Take-home "Little Jack Horner"

Copy the "Little Jack Horner" illustrations from page 35 onto card stock and distribute. Color, cut out, and assemble the pieces at the end of storytime, or encourage the families to do so at home. Glue or tape the pie crust pocket directly over the pie on Jack's lap, making sure to leave the top of the pie pocket open. Fasten Jack's elbow at the dot with a metal brad fastener or knotted yarn. Make a sample of the take-home version, and demonstrate singing or saying the rhyme using the small pieces. (Families may affix sticky-back magnet material to pieces for playtime use on a magnetic surface such as a cookie sheet or the refrigerator if desired. Be aware of choking hazard considerations for younger children.)

Additional Extension Ideas

Note: For all craft activities, provide materials for adult attendees as well as children. Encourage children and adults to talk together about what they are making, and to use the completed crafts to retell or act out the rhyme.

- Make a Little Jack Horner's Pie craft. Purchase small plastic paper plates or small-sized disposable aluminum patty pans as pie tins. Turn the plates or pans upside down on tan "crust-colored" felt and trace. Cut out the felt circles, then cut a medium-sized "X" in the middle of each circle. Glue the felt circles around the top edge of the plate or pan to form the top crust of the pie. Put various things into the pies that can be pulled out through the "X," such as giant purple pom-pom plums, cutout paper fruit or objects, and so forth. Say the rhyme with the little pie props.

- Play with the words in the rhyme and change them. Use props to dramatize. For example, have Little Jack Horner pull an apple, pear, pumpkin, cherry, blueberry, and so forth from his pie.

- Talk about: If you could have any kind of pie in the whole world, what kind of pie would you want to eat? Do you think you would want a candy pie? A Cheerios pie? An ice cream pie? An apple pie? What kinds of pie have you tasted before? Taste tiny samples

of various pies. Make sure in advance that none of the children have any food allergies or restrictions.

- Since Little Jack Horner pulled a "plum" from his pie, sample a few slices of a fresh plum. Show a fresh plum together with a prune to show what plums become as they dry out.

- If you have adequate time and are feeling brave, demonstrate making a real pie! Make sure the children are positioned so they can all see clearly. Prepare the pie crust dough and filling ahead of time, but demonstrate how you would measure the ingredients and stir them together. Roll out the crust and place it into the pie tin, add filling, and roll a second crust for the top. Poke holes in the crust for air to escape. Taste tiny samples of a finished pie, making sure in advance that none of the children have any food allergies or restrictions.

- Make a Pull Out a Plum From the Pie craft. Complete instructions are included in the book *Crafts From Your Favorite Nursery Rhymes* by Kathy Ross (Millbrook Press, 2002).

- Read *The Apple Pie Tree* by Zoe Hall (Scholastic, 1996). It describes an apple tree as it grows leaves and flowers and then produces fruit. An industrious pair of robins simultaneously makes a nest, lays eggs, and raises a family in the tree's branches. Includes a recipe for apple pie.

- Read *Pie in the Sky* by Lois Ehlert (Harcourt, 2004). A father and child watch the cherry tree in their backyard, waiting until there are ripe cherries to bake in a pie. A cherry pie recipe is included.

- Share "Little Jack Horner and Little Tommy Tucker" "in two voices" from *You Read to Me, I'll Read to You: Very Short Mother Goose Tales to Read Together* by Mary Ann Hoberman; illustrated by Michael Emberley (Little, Brown and Company, 2005). Before you begin, familiarize the children with the standard version of "Little Tommy Tucker" from a classic Mother Goose rhyme book.

- Make the shapes of "J" and "j" using string, pipe cleaners, or clay.

Little Jack Horner

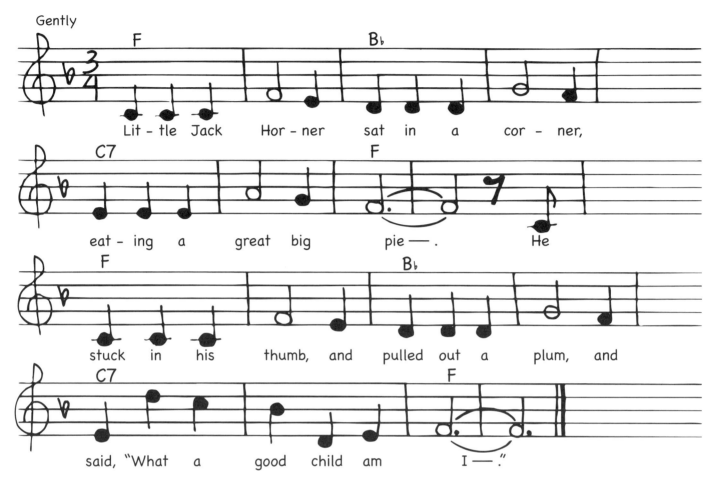

Gently

F

B♭

Lit - tle Jack Hor - ner sat in a cor - ner,

C7

F

eat - ing a great big pie —. He

F

B♭

stuck in his thumb, and pulled out a plum, and

C7

F

said, "What a good child am I —."

Take-home Little Jack Horner

Little Jack Horner

Sat in a corner,

Eating a great big pie.

He stuck in his thumb,

And pulled out a plum,

And said, "What a good child am I!"

Mistress Mary

> "Mary, Mary, quite contrary,
>
> How does your garden grow?"
>
> "With silver bells and cockleshells,
>
> And pretty maids all in a row."

Variants

The rhyme is relatively uniform in most of its recent renditions. A few replace the opening "Mary, Mary, quite contrary" with "Mistress Mary, quite contrary" or "Mrs. Mary, quite contrary." One early version gives the last line as "And so my Garden grows," while several others respectively conclude: "With lady bells all in a row"; "And columbines in a row"; "And cowslips all a row."

History

Scholars have debated the meaning of this rhyme without much success. The "silver bells" may be the white flowers of the small "silverbell" tree, or could refer to a custom of hanging silver bells on tree branches to tinkle in the wind. Some believe that the rhyme describes the Roman Catholic Church, with Mary representing the Virgin, the silver bells as church bells, and the pretty maids depicting the nuns. Others think it refers to Mary, Queen of Scots (1542–1587) and her ladies in waiting. Light-hearted, Catholic Mary was often seen as "contrary" by many of the court's pious Protestants.

Musical Notation

See musical notation on page 42.

Preparing and Using the Mother Goose Rhyme Time Pieces

"Mistress Mary" pieces:

- Mary
- Group of silver bell flowers
- Row of cockleshell seashells
- Row of girl-like flowers
- "Mary Mary Quite Contrary" poster

Organize the "Mistress Mary" rhyme pieces ahead of time in the order in which they appear in the rhyme: the "pretty maid" girl-like flowers on the bottom of the stack, the cockleshell seashells on top of them, the silver bell flowers on top of the seashells, and Mary on the very top. Hide the stack out of sight.

Before sharing the rhyme, place the poster on an easel so the audience can see it clearly. Hold Mary in one hand as you sing or say the rhyme. With your other hand, hold up each group of flowers or shells and then put it down again as you sing, or affix the pieces successively to a large Velcro or magnet board. If you wish to incorporate motions or use a musical instrument for accompaniment, you can point to each piece on the board in turn as you lead the group in the actions or play and sing the song.

Utilize the sections of Mother Goose Rhyme Time that work best for you and your storytime group or classroom. Experiment with new ideas and techniques. Practice ahead of time so you feel comfortable with the material and can focus on the audience rather than on trying to remember how you intended to share the rhyme.

Storytime

Share "Mistress Mary" as a song or chant; rocking back and forth, bouncing, patting your lap, or clapping to keep a rhythm. Sing or say the rhyme fast and slow, loudly and quietly. Incorporate movements as desired. Encourage the children's caregivers to adapt motions or make up new ones as appropriate for their child; many different actions are possible. Here are a few options:

Babies (*Sitting on caregivers' laps*)

> "Mary, Mary, quite contrary,
> (*Bounce baby.*)
> How does your garden grow?"
> (*Hands out, questioning.*)
> "With silver bells and cockleshells,
> (*Bounce baby.*)
> And pretty maids all in a row."
> (*Lift baby UP in the air.*)

Older Children (*Standing*)

> "Mary, Mary, quite contrary,
> (*Wave hands high, back and forth.*)
> How does your garden grow?"
> (*Hands out, questioning.*)
> "With silver bells and cockleshells,
> (*Swoop hands out in bell shape; hold out cupped hands.*)
> And pretty maids all in a row.
> (*Curtsey or bow.*)

Early Literacy Activities

Consider integrating one or several of the activities or techniques suggested below as you share the nursery rhyme. All activities should be approached in a fun and playful manner, encouraging curiosity and allowing for children's individual differences. **Note:** Be aware of children's developmental stages and focus on the activities that are appropriate for the ages and stages of your group. The suggestions provided are intended to give you a variety of ideas

to work with over time. You will not incorporate all of the techniques at once. Share one rhyme several times during a single storytime, and repeat the same rhyme over several storytimes. Try different activities to highlight a different skill during each storytime.

Print Motivation (*Encourage interest in and excitement about reading and books.*)

- Say the words rhythmically and with enthusiasm, conveying your enjoyment of the rhyme.

- Create a voice for Mary, and change your tone and facial expression as appropriate to the context.

- Repeat the rhyme several times together with the children, encouraging their own enjoyment and internalization of its lively rhythms.

Language and Vocabulary (*Introduce and explain new words or new meanings to familiar words.*)

- Use the rhyme pieces to illustrate and help explain language and vocabulary. Say: "This girl's name is Mary (*point to Mary*). We call her 'Mistress Mary' in the rhyme, which is like saying 'Miss Mary.' She is quite, or very, contrary. What does it mean to be 'contrary'? It can mean that you just like to do things differently, opposite, or 'contrary' to what is usually done or expected; or it can mean that you are being willful or naughty on purpose. Do you sometimes feel 'contrary'? Someone who is often contrary is called a 'contrarian.' We are asking Mary about her garden, and she tells us that it is growing with silver bells, which probably means bell-shaped flowers; and cockleshells, which are seashells she put along the path to make it pretty; and pretty maids, which probably means girl-like flowers, all in a row."

- Talk or sing about the illustrations: "I see a girl." "I see flowers." Pause for the children to name the object to which you are pointing: "I see a _____." Expand on descriptive features of the illustrations to build vocabulary and encourage the children's awareness of and attention to details. For example: "I see a girl. A girl wearing a hat and holding a watering can."

Phonological Awareness (*Play with rhymes, practice breaking words apart and putting them back together, and listen for beginning sounds and alliteration.*)

- Explain that rhyming words sound the same at the end. Play an "oddity task" game. For example, which word does not rhyme? Grow, bells, row. (*Answer: bells.*) Which word sounds different at the beginning? Mary, maids, does. (*Answer: does.*) Which word sounds different at the end? Garden, bells, maids. (*Answer: garden.*)

- Blend word parts in a variety of ways.

  Syllables: sil … ver. What's the word? (*Silver.*)

  Onset sound: /r/ … ow. What's the word? (*Row.*) What other words start with /r/?

  Phoneme by phoneme (for older children, in primary grades): /w/-/i/-/th/. What's the word? (*With.*)

- Practice segmenting or "stretching" the nursery rhyme words (for older children, in primary grades). Show the children a rubber band and stretch it out and in. As you stretch the rubber band out longer, you can see all of its parts more clearly. Explain that you can also stretch words, so that you can hear each individual sound (phoneme) in the word. Stretch the word "and": /a/-/n/-/d/. Sometimes one phoneme is represented by more than one letter, such as in the word "bells": /b/-/e/-/ll/-/s/. "Bells" contains four phonemes. Stretch other nursery rhyme words.

- Clap words: Clap once for each word in the rhyme, following the poster. Introduce variety by stomping feet or jumping once for each word.

- Clap syllables: Older children can learn to clap once for each syllable in the rhyme. Practice with one word at a time as the children begin to understand the concept. For example: Mar-y (2 claps); Mar-y (2 claps); quite (1 clap); con-tra-ry (3 claps); How (1 clap); does (1 clap); your (1 clap); gar-den (2 claps); grow (1 clap)? Introduce variety by stomping feet or jumping to the syllables.

Print Awareness (*Notice print and know how to handle books and follow the written word on a page.*)

- Point to the "Mistress Mary" poster. Say: "Our nursery rhyme is written right up here. I'll read it aloud, and then we'll say it again together." Follow the text of the rhyme with your finger as you read the poster, from left to right.

- Occasionally turn the poster upside down or sideways and see if the children detect the problem.

Narrative Skills (*Practice retelling stories or events, sequencing the order in which events happened, and adding descriptions.*)

- Talk and ask two or three open-ended questions about the rhyme and the objects and characters in it, and allow the children to ask questions. Avoid asking yes/no questions unless there is a specific purpose in doing so. Qualify questions by including the phrase "do you think," as in "Why do you think …?" or "What do you think …?" This type of question does not have a "right" answer that children are afraid they will get wrong. For example: Why do you think we are calling Mary "contrary"? What might she have done or be doing that is contrary, or the opposite of what is expected? What might be in her garden besides the silver bells and cockleshells and pretty maids? Do you think there are more flowers? What kind of flowers? What colors do you think they are? Do you think she has planted some vegetables? What kind of vegetables? What are some of the things that seeds need to help them grow after they are planted?

Letter Knowledge—Letter M (*Learn to recognize and identify letters, knowing that they have different names and sounds and that the same letter can look different.*)

- Show a large-size cutout or magnet-backed foam letter "M" and "m" (see Resources). Point to the capital "M" letters that begin the words "Mistress" and "Mary" in the title of your poster. Say: "Here is the letter M—a big uppercase, or capital M." Draw the capital letter "M" in the air as a group. Point to a small letter "m" on the poster within the

rhyme's text. Say: "Here is also the letter m—a small, lowercase m." Draw a lowercase "m" in the air as a group. Make the /M/ sound and say: "M is for Mistress Mary; M is for Man; M is for Moon; M is for Mouse; M is for Milk; M is for Mail; M is for Mommy; M is for Me." Encourage the audience to repeat each phrase after you. Include three or four examples.

- Demonstrate making the shapes of "M" and "m" using string or pipe cleaners.

Parent/Caregiver Connection

- Reinforce the parent/caregiver's key role in their child's early literacy development through comfortable, relaxed times together with songs, rhymes, and books. Emphasize fun and enjoyment as the goals.

- Encourage caregivers to participate during storytime and incorporate "Mistress Mary" at home during play and reading times. Select one of the "Mistress Mary" early literacy activities that you share together during storytime, and briefly explain how the activity supports children's early literacy development. Suggest repeating the activity at home. Try different activities to highlight different skills during each storytime.

- Share information about Dialogic, or "Hear and Say" Reading (see Resources). Encourage parents and caregivers to individually discuss the day's rhyme, its characters, and events in an open-ended way with their children, following the child's interest while affirming and expanding upon their answers. For example, point to Mary in "Mistress Mary" and ask, "Who is this?" Child: "A girl." Follow up with positive affirmation, and enlarge: "Yes, it's a girl named Mary. What is she doing?" Child: "Flowers." Expand: "Yes, she is watering the flowers in her garden." Help the child repeat longer phrases. Ask open-ended questions such as: "What do you see in this picture?" Build on the things that catch the child's interest. This type of positive, interactive discussion around familiar rhymes and books helps improve early language development, communication, and parent/child relationships.

Take-home "Mistress Mary"

Copy the "Mistress Mary" illustrations from pages 43–44 onto card stock and distribute. Color and cut out the pieces at the end of storytime, or encourage the families to do so at home. Make a sample of the take-home version, and demonstrate singing or saying the rhyme using the small pieces. (Families may affix sticky-back magnet material to pieces for playtime use on a magnetic surface such as a cookie sheet or the refrigerator if desired. Be aware of choking hazard considerations for younger children.)

Additional Extension Ideas

Note: For all craft activities, provide materials for adult attendees as well as children. Encourage children and adults to talk together about what they are making, and to use the completed crafts to retell or act out the rhyme.

- Show the pictures from several different nursery rhyme books that illustrate "Mistress Mary," and repeat the rhyme together with each new illustration. Talk about the differences between the various illustrations.

- Fill a plastic cup with potting soil for each child, and plant some real flower seeds! Choose seeds that sprout fairly quickly, such as zinnias or marigolds.

- Plant a nursery rhyme flower garden. Include flowers such as lily-of-the-valley for Mary's "silver bells," and hollyhocks as her "pretty maids." Lambs' ear is a lovely soft tactile addition (for "Little Bo-Peep" and "Baa Baa Black Sheep") and cleome is also called "spider flower" (for "Little Miss Muffet"). Outline the sections with shells like Mistress Mary did in her garden.

- Cut out paper flowers and shells, and glue them to brown paper to make Mistress Mary's garden.

- Make a string of connected paper doll "pretty maid" flowers for Mistress Mary's garden.

- Make a playtime "Mistress Mary" garden from thick foam (available at fabric stores) and silk flowers. Cut the foam to fit into a

long, narrow plastic planter. Cut "Xs" into the foam, and paint it brown. Allow the paint to dry completely, then hot glue the foam into the planter. Plant, "water" (with an empty watering can), and pick the silk flowers for creative play.

- Make Flower Paper Bag Puppets to grow in a pretend garden. Act out the process of seeds growing into beautiful flowers with creative dramatics. Each child hides his or her flower puppet as a curled-up seed until they are "watered" with an empty watering can and a large sun stick puppet is waved over them. See A *Pocketful of Puppets: Mother Goose* by Tamara Hunt and Nancy Renfro (Nancy Renfro Studios, 1998).

- Make Mistress Mary's Bouquet. Complete instructions are included in the book *Crafts From Your Favorite Nursery Rhymes* by Kathy Ross (Millbrook Press, 2002).

- Read *Contrary Mary* by Anita Jeram (Candlewick Press, 1995). Contrary Mary the mouse decides to do the opposite of what she is supposed to do. When her mother begins to do the same thing, however, Mary has a change of heart.

- Read *Planting a Rainbow* written and illustrated by Lois Ehlert (Harcourt, 1988). A mother and child plant a rainbow of flowers in the family garden.

- Make the shapes of "M" and "m" using string, pipe cleaners, or clay.

Mistress Mary

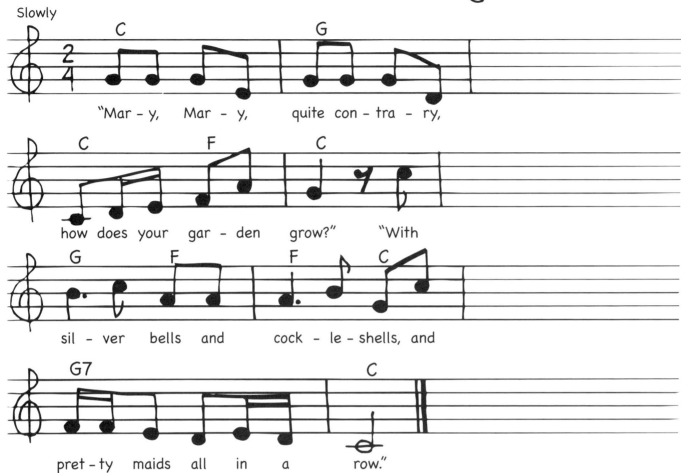

Slowly

C

"Mar - y, Mar - y, quite con - tra - ry,

C   F   C

how does your gar - den grow?" "With

G   F   F   C

sil - ver bells and cock - le - shells, and

G7   C

pret - ty maids all in a row."

Take-home Mistress Mary

"Mary, Mary, quite contrary,
How does your garden grow?"
"With silver bells and cockleshells,
And pretty maids all in a row."

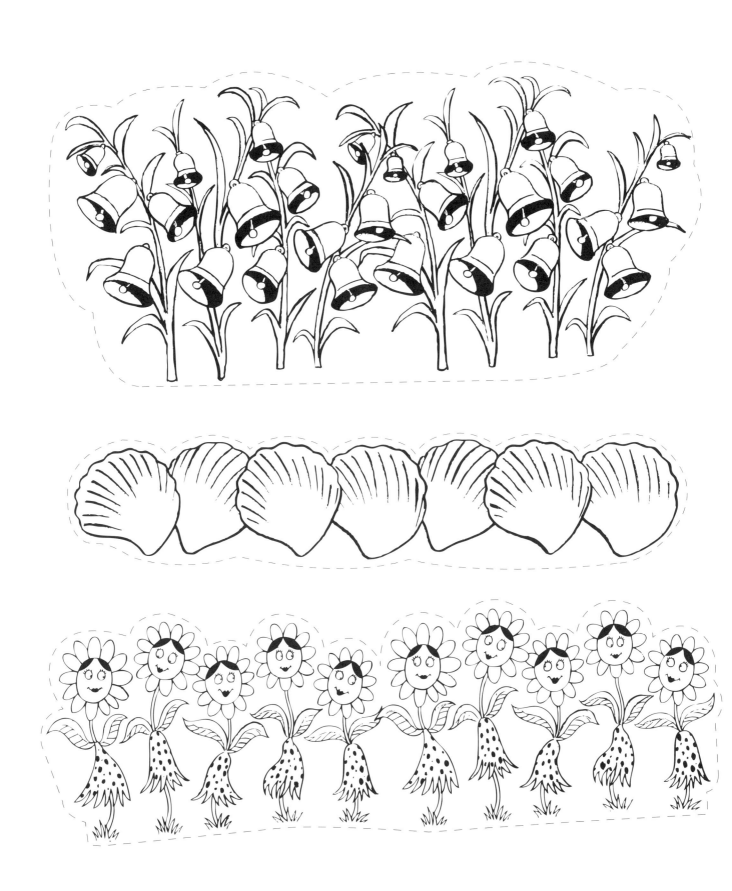

There Was an Old Woman Lived Under a Hill

> There was an old woman
> Lived under a hill,
> And if she's not gone
> She lives there still.

Variants

Some versions add the couplet "Baked apples she sold, and cranberry pies, And she's the old woman that never told lies."

History

This sort of "self-evident proposition," which stated the obvious in a silly manner, was popular in the seventeenth and eighteenth centuries.

Musical Notation

See musical notation on page 50.

Preparing and Using the Mother Goose Rhyme Time Pieces

"There Was an Old Woman Lived Under a Hill" pieces:

* Double-layered hill with old woman and her house

* "There Was an Old Woman Lived Under a Hill" poster

Before sharing the rhyme, place the poster on an easel so the audience can see it clearly. Hold up the hill in one or both hands as you say or sing the rhyme, or affix it to a large Velcro or magnet board. When you say "under a hill," point "under" the hill. At the very end of the rhyme, swivel the top hill layer up and out to one side to reveal the old woman and her house. If you wish to incorporate motions, lead the audience in the actions and then dramatically reveal the old woman each time you end the rhyme. Pause slightly before moving the hill front, as if she might not be there this time around. You can even pretend to listen for her!

Utilize the sections of Mother Goose Rhyme Time that work best for you and your storytime group or classroom. Experiment with new ideas and techniques. Practice ahead of time so you feel comfortable with the material and can focus on the audience rather than on trying to remember how you intended to share the rhyme.

Storytime

Share "There Was an Old Woman Lived Under a Hill" as a song or chant; bouncing, patting your lap, or clapping to keep a rhythm. Sing or say the rhyme quickly and slowly, loudly and quietly. Add movements as desired. Encourage the children's caregivers to adapt motions or make up new ones as appropriate for their child. Many different actions are possible. Here are a few options:

Babies (*Sitting on caregivers' laps*)

There was an old woman
(*Bounce baby gently throughout the rhyme.*)
Lived under a hill,
And if she's not gone
She lives there still.
(*Lift baby UP in the air.*)

Older Children (*Standing*)

There was an old woman
(*Crouch down, as if hiding.*)
Lived under a hill,
And if she's not gone
She lives there still.
(*Pop up with hands raised high.*)

Early Literacy Activities

Consider integrating one or several of the activities or techniques suggested below as you share the nursery rhyme. All activities should be approached in a fun and playful manner, encouraging curiosity and allowing for children's individual differences. **Note:** Be aware of children's developmental stages and focus on the activities that are appropriate for the ages and stages of your group. The suggestions provided are intended to give you a variety of ideas to work with over time. You will not incorporate all of the techniques at once. Share one rhyme several times during a single storytime, and repeat the same rhyme over several storytimes. Try different activities to highlight a different skill during each storytime.

Print Motivation (*Encourage interest in and excitement about reading and books.*)

- Say the words rhythmically and with enthusiasm, conveying your enjoyment of the rhyme.

- Repeat the rhyme several times together with the children, encouraging their own enjoyment and internalization of its lively rhythms.

Language and Vocabulary (*Introduce and explain new words or new meanings to familiar words.*)

- Use the rhyme pieces to illustrate and help explain language and vocabulary. Say: "There was an old woman (*point to the old woman*) who lived under a hill (*point to the hill*). If she's not gone, she lives there still, which means if she's not gone, she still lives there."

- Talk or sing about the illustrations: "I see a hill." "I see a tree." Pause for the children to name the object to which you are pointing: "I see a _____." Expand on descriptive features of the illustrations to build vocabulary and encourage the children's awareness of and attention to details: "I see a hill. A hill with a tree and a goat at the very top."

Phonological Awareness (*Play with rhymes, practice breaking words apart and putting them back together, and listen for beginning sounds and alliteration.*)

- Play with the words, objects, and activities in the rhyme and change them. Use puppets or props to dramatize. For example:

There was an old woman
Who lived in a house,
She cleaned every Monday,
And had a pet mouse.

There was an old woman
Who rode on a train,
She had an umbrella,
In case it might rain.

- Explain that rhyming words sound the same at the end. "Hill" and "still"; "house" and "mouse"; and "train" and "rain" are all rhyming word pairs. Try pausing just before the end of a rhyming pair and encourage the children to supply the rhyming word (such as "mouse" and "rain" above) with the support of visual clues or context, or simply through the sounds suggested by the rhyme.

- Blend word parts in a variety of ways.

Syllables: wom ... an. What's the word? (*Woman.*)

<u>Onset sound:</u> /h/ ... ill. What's the word? *(Hill.)* What other words start with /h/?

<u>Phoneme by phoneme (for older children, in primary grades):</u> /o/-/l/-/d/. What's the word? *(Old.)*

- Practice segmenting or "stretching" the nursery rhyme words (for older children, in primary grades). Show the children a rubber band and stretch it out and in. As you stretch the rubber band out longer, you can see all of its parts more clearly. Explain that you can also stretch words, so that you can hear each individual sound (phoneme) in the word. Stretch the word "old": /o/-/l/-/d/. Sometimes one phoneme is represented by more than one letter, such as in the word "hill": /h/-/i/-/ll/. "Hill" contains three phonemes. Stretch other nursery rhyme words.

- Clap words: Clap once for each word in the rhyme, following the poster. Introduce variety by stomping feet or jumping once for each word.

- Clap syllables: Older children can learn to clap once for each syllable in the rhyme. Practice with one word at a time as the children begin to understand the concept. For example: There (1 clap); was (1 clap); an (1 clap); old (1 clap); wom-an (2 claps); Lived (1 clap); un-der (2 claps); a (1 clap); hill (1 clap). Introduce variety by stomping feet or jumping to the syllables.

Print Awareness *(Notice print and know how to handle books and follow the written word on a page.)*

- Point to the "There Was an Old Woman Lived Under a Hill" poster. Say: "Our nursery rhyme is written right up here. I'll read it aloud, and then we'll say it again together." Follow the text of the rhyme with your finger as you read the poster, from left to right.

- Occasionally turn the poster upside down or sideways and see if the children detect the problem.

Narrative Skills *(Practice retelling stories or events, sequencing the order in which events happened, and adding descriptions.)*

- Talk and ask two or three open-ended questions about the rhyme and the objects and characters in it, and allow the children to ask questions. Avoid asking yes/no questions unless there is a specific purpose in doing so. Qualify questions by including the phrase "do you think," as in "Why do you think ...?" or "What do you think ...?" This type of question does not have a "right" answer that children are afraid they will get wrong. For example: Why do you think the old woman lived under the hill? Do you think anyone else lived there with her? If yes, who else? Do you think that she had any pets? If yes, what kind of pets?

- If you have a small enough group and adequate time, act out "There Was an Old Woman Lived Under a Hill" with creative dramatics. Make a hill house by draping a blanket over a table. Have several children at a time hide under the table as the Old Women/Old Men while the other children chant the rhyme. Make sure that each child gets to play both roles.

Letter Knowledge—Letter W *(Learn to recognize and identify letters, knowing that they have different names and sounds and that the same letter can look different.)*

- Show a large-size cutout or magnet-backed foam letter "W" and "w" (see Resources). Point to the capital "W" letter that begins the word "Woman" in the title of your poster. Say: "Here is the letter W—a big uppercase, or capital W." Draw the capital letter "W" in the air as a group. Point to a small letter "w" on the poster within the rhyme's text. Say: "Here is also the letter w—a small, lowercase w." Draw a lowercase "w" in the air as a group. Make the /W/ sound and say: "W is for Woman; W is for Wind; W is for Water; W is for Wish; W is for Window; W is for Wait; W is for Wash; W is for Worm; W is for Want." Encourage the audience to repeat each phrase after you. Include three or four examples.

- Demonstrate making the shapes of "W" and "w" using string or pipe cleaners.

Parent/Caregiver Connection

- Reinforce the parent/caregiver's key role in their child's early literacy development through comfortable, relaxed times together with songs, rhymes, and books. Emphasize fun and enjoyment as the goals.

- Encourage caregivers to participate during storytime and to incorporate "There Was an Old Woman Lived Under a Hill" at home during play and reading times. Select one of the "There Was an Old Woman Lived Under a Hill" early literacy activities that you share together during storytime, and briefly explain how the activity supports children's early literacy development. Suggest repeating the activity at home. Try different activities to highlight different skills during each storytime.

- Share information about Dialogic, or "Hear and Say" Reading (see Resources). Encourage parents and caregivers to individually discuss the day's rhyme, its characters, and events in an open-ended way with their children, following the child's interest while affirming and expanding upon their answers. For example, point to the hill in "There Was an Old Woman Lived Under a Hill" and ask, "What is this?" Child: "Hill." Follow up with positive affirmation, and enlarge: "Yes, it's a hill, with a tree on the very top! What else do you see?" Child: "Rock." Expand: "Yes, there are rocks along the road that is leading around the hill." Help the child repeat longer phrases. Ask open-ended questions such as: "What do you see in this picture?" Build on the things that catch the child's interest. This type of positive, interactive discussion around familiar rhymes and books helps improve early language development, communication, and parent/child relationships.

Take-home "There Was an Old Woman Lived Under a Hill"

Copy the "There Was an Old Woman Lived Under a Hill" illustrations from pages 51–52 onto card stock and distribute. Color, cut out, and assemble the pieces at the end of storytime, or encourage the families to do so at home. Fasten the plain hill front to the back hill piece at the dot. Use a metal brad fastener or knotted yarn so that the front can swivel out to the side. Make a sample of the take-home version, and demonstrate singing or saying the rhyme using the small pieces. (Families may affix sticky-back magnet material to pieces for playtime use on a magnetic surface such as a cookie sheet or the refrigerator if desired. Be aware of choking hazard considerations for younger children.)

Additional Extension Ideas

Note: For all craft activities, provide materials for adult attendees as well as children. Encourage children and adults to talk together about what they are making, and to use the completed crafts to retell or act out the rhyme.

- Show the pictures from several different nursery rhyme books that illustrate "There Was an Old Woman Lived Under a Hill," and repeat the rhyme together with each new illustration. Talk about the differences between the various illustrations.

- Talk about: Where do people live? Look at photographs of different kinds of houses throughout the world, and discuss why the houses are built differently. For example, houses in coastal areas are often up on stilts due to regular flooding. Read *Houses and Homes* by Ann Morris (Lothrop, Lee & Shepard Books, 1992).

- Talk about: Why did the old woman live under a hill? The earth is a good insulator; it can help keep your house warm in winter and cool in the summer. Show photographs of earth houses.

- Read *We Were Tired Of Living In A House* by Liesel Moak Skorpen; illustrated by Joe Cepeda (Putnam, 1999). Four children, a cat, and a dog move to a tree, a raft, a cave, and finally the seashore. They enjoy each new home until they discover its inevitable drawbacks.

- If you have a small enough group so everyone can see the detailed lift-the-flap illustrations, read *The House That Jill Built* by Phyllis Root; illustrated by Delphine Durand (Candlewick Press, 2005). Numerous nursery rhyme and storybook characters show up at Jill's small cozy house with demands for rooms with special amenities. Jill obligingly complies, enlarging her home as she builds each of them their own specialized quarters. She ends up building herself a new small cozy house!

- Make construction paper houses for the old woman in the rhyme and her friends.

- If you are feeling brave, build three-dimensional houses from graham crackers and marshmallow crème or sugar frosting.

- Talk about: Where do animals live? Look at photographs of different kinds of animal homes throughout the world.

- Read *Home for a Bunny* by Margaret Wise Brown; pictures by Garth Williams (Golden Books, 1988, 1984, 1960, 1956). A bunny hops down the road looking for a home. A robin, frog, and groundhog all tell him where they live, but he realizes none of their homes would be right for a bunny. At last he joins another little bunny in a perfect home under the ground.

- Sing "Do You Know Where I Live?" in *Storytimes for Two-Year-Olds* by Judy Nichols, second edition (American Library Assn., 1998), using props and puppets to dramatize.

- Make the shapes of "W" and "w" using string, pipe cleaners, or clay.

There Was an Old Woman Lived Under A Hill

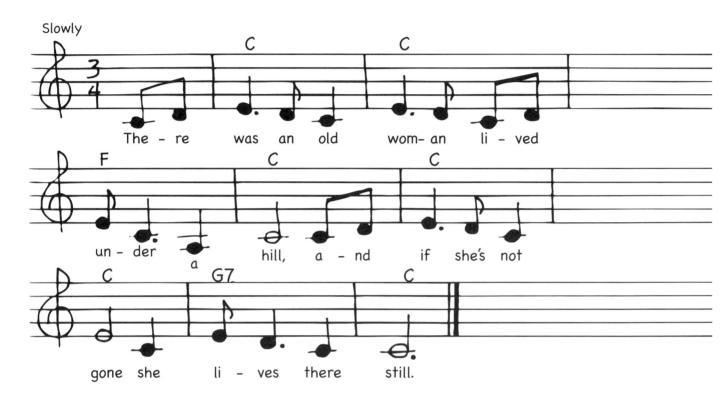

Slowly

There was an old wom-an li-ved
un-der a hill, a-nd if she's not
gone she li-ves there still.

Take-home There Was an Old Woman Lived Under a Hill

> There was an old woman
> Lived under a hill,
> And if she's not gone
> She lives there still.

Rub-A-Dub Dub

> Rub-a-dub dub,
>
> Three men in a tub,
>
> And who do you think they be?
>
> The butcher, the baker, the candlestick-maker,
>
> They all set out to sea.

Variants

There are several fairly distinct versions of this rhyme, including the common "Throw them out, knaves all three!" as the last line. Other variants include "brewer" instead of "butcher," and references to a rotten or "mealy" potato:

> Rub-a-dub dub,
> Three men in a tub,
> And how do you think they got there?
> The butcher, the baker, the candlestick-maker,
> They all jumped out of a rotten potato,
> 'Twas enough to make a man stare.

History

In the earliest recorded versions of the rhyme (circa 1798), the three people in the tub are actually three maids lounging in a tub as a village fair sideshow. The butcher, baker, and candlestick-maker are apparently there as onlookers, a questionable pastime for supposedly respectable tradesmen.

> Hey! Rub-a-dub, ho! Rub-a-dub,
> Three maids in a tub,
> And who do you think were there?
> The butcher, the baker, the candlestick-maker,
> And all of them gone to the fair.

Musical Notation

See musical notation on page 58.

Preparing and Using the Mother Goose Rhyme Time Pieces

"Rub-A-Dub Dub" pieces:

- Three men in washtub

- "Rub-A-Dub Dub" poster

Before sharing the rhyme, place the poster on an easel so the audience can see it clearly. Hold the three men in the washtub piece in one or both hands throughout the rhyme, or affix the piece to a large Velcro or magnet board. Point to each character as you sing or say the rhyme, then rock the washtub as if it is a boat as "they all set out to sea." If you wish to incorporate motions or use a musical instrument for accompaniment, point to each character on the board in turn as you lead the group in the actions or play and sing the song.

Utilize the sections of Mother Goose Rhyme Time that work best for you and your storytime group or classroom. Experiment with new ideas and techniques. Practice ahead of time so you feel comfortable with the material and can focus on the audience rather than on trying to remember how you intended to share the rhyme.

Storytime

Share "Rub-A-Dub Dub" as a song or chant; rocking back and forth, bouncing, patting your lap, or clapping to keep a rhythm. Sing or say the rhyme quickly and slowly, loudly and quietly. Incorporate movements as desired. Encourage the children's caregivers to adapt motions or make up new ones as appropriate for their child; many different actions are possible. Here are a few options:

Babies (*Sitting on caregivers' laps*)

> Rub-a-dub dub,
> (*Gently scrub baby as if bathing.*)
> Three men in a tub,
> And who do you think they be?
> (*Hands out, questioning.*)
> The butcher, the baker,
> The candlestick-maker,
> (*Gently tap belly three times.*)
> They all set out to sea.
> (*Rock baby back and forth.*)

Older Children (*Standing or sitting*)

> Rub-a-dub dub,
> (*Scrub as if washing yourself all over.*)
> Three men in a tub,
> And who do you think they be?
> (*Hands out, questioning.*)
> The butcher, the baker,
> The candlestick-maker
> (*Hold up one, two, three fingers.*)
> They all set out to sea.
> (*Cup hands together to form sailing boat.*)

Early Literacy Activities

Consider integrating one or several of the activities or techniques suggested below as you share the nursery rhyme. All activities should be approached in a fun and playful manner, encouraging curiosity and allowing for children's individual differences. **Note:** Be aware of children's developmental stages and focus on the activities that are appropriate for the ages and stages of your group. The suggestions provided are intended to give you a variety of ideas to work with over time. You will not incorporate

all of the techniques at once. Share one rhyme several times during a single storytime, and repeat the same rhyme over several storytimes. Try different activities to highlight a different skill during each storytime.

Print Motivation (*Encourage interest in and excitement about reading and books.*)

- Say the words rhythmically and with enthusiasm, conveying your enjoyment of the rhyme.

- Repeat the rhyme several times together with the children, encouraging their own enjoyment and internalization of its lively rhythms.

Language and Vocabulary (*Introduce and explain new words or new meanings to familiar words.*)

- Use the rhyme pieces to illustrate and help explain language and vocabulary. Say: "In our rhyme, there are three men (*point to the three men*) in a tub (*point to the tub*). It is like a big washtub, or a big bathtub. Let's count the men: one, two, three (*point to each man in turn as you count together*). Here is the butcher (*point to the butcher*). His job is getting meat ready for people to cook and eat. Here is the baker (*point to the baker*). His job is to bake bread and cakes and cookies for people to eat. Here is the candlestick-maker (*point to the candlestick-maker*). His job is to make candles and candlesticks for people to buy and light their houses. They are all going out to sea in their tub!"

- Talk or sing about the illustrations: "I see the butcher." "I see the baker." Pause for the children to name the person to whom you are pointing: "I see the _____." Expand on descriptive features of the illustrations to build vocabulary and encourage the children's awareness of and attention to details: "I see a man. A man holding a candlestick with three candles."

Phonological Awareness (*Play with rhymes, practice breaking words apart and putting them back together, and listen for beginning sounds and alliteration.*)

- Play with the words, objects, and names in the rhyme and change them. Use puppets or props to dramatize. For example:

Rub-a-dub dee,
Three cats in a tree,
And who do you think they are?
The three little kittens who lost their mittens!
They all drove away in a car.

- Explain that rhyming words sound the same at the end. "Dub" and "tub"; "be" and "sea"; "dee" and "tree"; and "are" and "car" are all rhyming word pairs. Try pausing just before the end of a rhyming pair and encourage the children to supply the rhyming word (such as "tree" and "car" above) with the support of visual clues or context, or simply through the sounds suggested by the rhyme.

- Play an "oddity task" game. For example, which word does not rhyme? Be, sea, men. *(Answer: men.)* Which word sounds different at the beginning? Maker, butcher, baker. *(Answer: maker.)* Which word sounds different at the end? Set, tub, out. *(Answer: tub.)*

- Blend word parts in a variety of ways.

  Syllables: bak … er. What's the word? *(Baker.)*

  Onset sound: /t/ … ub. What's the word? *(Tub.)* What other words start with /t/?

  Phoneme by phoneme (for older children, in primary grades): /m/-/e/-/n/. What's the word? *(Men.)*

- Practice segmenting or "stretching" the nursery rhyme words (for older children, in primary grades). Show the children a rubber band and stretch it out and in. As you stretch the rubber band out longer, you can see all of its parts more clearly. Explain that you can also stretch words, so that you can hear each individual sound (phoneme) in the word. Stretch the word "tub": /t/-/u/-/b/. Sometimes one phoneme is represented by more than one letter, such as in the word "three": /th/-/r/-/ee/. "Three" contains three phonemes. Stretch other nursery rhyme words.

- Clap words: Clap once for each word in the rhyme, following the poster. Introduce variety by stomping feet or jumping once for each word.

- Clap syllables: Older children can learn to clap once for each syllable in the rhyme. Practice with one word at a time as the children begin to understand the concept. For example: Rub-a-dub dub (4 claps); Three (1 clap); men (1 clap); in (1 clap); a (1 clap); tub (1 clap). Introduce variety by stomping feet or jumping to the syllables.

Print Awareness *(Notice print and know how to handle books and follow the written word on a page.)*

- Point to the "Rub-A-Dub Dub" poster. Say: "Our nursery rhyme is written right up here. I'll read it aloud, and then we'll say it again together." Follow the text of the rhyme with your finger as you read the poster, from left to right.

- Occasionally turn the poster upside down or sideways and see if the children detect the problem.

Narrative Skills *(Practice retelling stories or events, sequencing the order in which events happened, and adding descriptions.)*

- Talk and ask two or three open-ended questions about the rhyme and the objects and characters in it, and allow the children to ask questions. Avoid asking yes/no questions unless there is a specific purpose in doing so. Qualify questions by including the phrase "do you think," as in "Why do you think …?" or "What do you think …?" This type of question does not have a "right" answer that children are afraid they will get wrong. For example: Where do you think the men are going in the tub? What do you think they will do when they get out to sea? Why do you think the men are going out to sea in a tub?

- If you have a small enough group and adequate time, act out "Rub-A-Dub Dub" with creative dramatics. Use a very large round plastic bin or a large cardboard box for the "tub." Have the children take turns sitting on the floor in the tub in groups of three as the 'three boys' or 'three girls' or 'three kids' in the tub. Have each child in the tub be the butcher, baker, or candlestick-maker, raising their hands as their occupation is called out in the rhyme. Have the children who are not in the tub sing or say the rhyme as a group, clapping to keep a rhythm. Make sure that each child gets to play both roles if desired, and to choose who or what they want to be.

Letter Knowledge—Letter D *(Learn to recognize and identify letters, knowing that they have different names and sounds and that the same letter can look different.)*

- Show a large-size cutout or magnet-backed foam letter "D" and "d" (see Resources). Point to the capital "D" letters that begin the words "Dub" in the title of your poster. Say: "Here is the letter D—a big uppercase, or capital D." Draw the capital letter "D" in the air as a group. Point to a small letter "d" on the poster within the rhyme's text. Say: "Here is also the letter d—a small, lowercase d." Draw a lowercase "d" in the air as a group. Make the /D/ sound and say: "D is for Dub; D is for Dinosaur; D is for Dog; D is for Duck; D is for Doughnut; D is for Dance; D is for Doll; D is for Door; D is for Daddy." Encourage the audience to repeat each phrase after you. Include three or four examples.

- Demonstrate making the shapes of "D" and "d" using string or pipe cleaners.

Parent/Caregiver Connection

- Reinforce the parent/caregiver's key role in their child's early literacy development through comfortable, relaxed times together with songs, rhymes, and books. Emphasize fun and enjoyment as the goals.

- Encourage caregivers to participate during storytime and to incorporate "Rub-A-Dub Dub" at home during play and reading times. Select one of the "Rub-A-Dub Dub" early literacy activities that you share together during storytime, and briefly explain how the activity supports children's early literacy development. Suggest repeating the activity at home. Try different activities to highlight different skills during each storytime.

- Share information about Dialogic, or "Hear and Say" Reading (see Resources). Encourage parents and caregivers to individually discuss the day's rhyme, its characters, and events in an open-ended way with their children, following the child's interest while affirming and expanding upon their answers. For example, point to the baker in "Rub-A-Dub Dub" and ask, "Who is this?" Child: "Baker." Follow up with positive affirmation, and enlarge: "Yes, it's the baker, wearing a chef's hat! What is he doing?" Child: "Boat." Expand: "Yes, he is using a big washtub for a boat to float out to sea with his friends." Help the child repeat longer phrases. Ask open-ended questions such as: "What do you see in this picture?" Build on the things that catch the child's interest. This type of positive, interactive discussion around familiar rhymes and books helps improve early language development, communication, and parent/child relationships.

Take-home "Rub-A-Dub Dub"

Copy the "Rub-A-Dub Dub" illustration from page 59 onto card stock and distribute. Color and cut out the piece at the end of storytime, or encourage the families to do so at home. Make a sample of the take-home version, and demonstrate singing or saying the rhyme using the small piece. (Families may affix sticky-back magnet material to pieces for playtime use on a magnetic surface such as a cookie sheet or the refrigerator if desired. Be aware of choking hazard considerations for younger children.)

Additional Extension Ideas

Note: For all craft activities, provide materials for adult attendees as well as children. Encourage children and adults to talk together about what they are making, and to use the completed crafts to retell or act out the rhyme.

- Show the pictures from several different nursery rhyme books that illustrate "Rub-A-Dub Dub" and repeat the rhyme together with each new illustration. Talk about the differences between the various illustrations.

- Make "Rub-A-Dub Dub" bathtub boats from plastic or Styrofoam bowls. Glue or tie a small piece of plastic bag to a craft stick for a sail and mast, and securely glue or tape the mast to the boat. Set the boats afloat in a large tub of shallow water. The water tub should be attended by an adult at all times, and should be emptied immediately when the sailing session is finished.

- Rhythmically chant the following bath time rhyme as a group with accompanying actions:

"Slippery Soap"
Slipp'ry, slipp'ry, slipp'ry soap
Now you see it, now you don't.
Slide it on your arms, 1–2–3,
Now your arms are slipp-er-y.

Slipp'ry, slipp'ry, slipp'ry soap
Now you see it, now you don't.
Slide it on your legs, 1–2–3,
Now your legs are slipp-er-y.

Slipp'ry, slipp'ry, slipp'ry soap
Now you see it, now you don't.

(Repeat the verse substituting different body parts.)

Adapted from *The Complete Book of Rhymes, Songs, Poems, Fingerplays and Chants*, compiled by Jackie Silberg and Pam Schiller (Gryphon House, 2002).

- Play the tune "Rub-a-Dub Dub / Row, Row, Row Your Boat" on the sound recording *Bathtime Magic* by Joanie Bartels (Discovery Music, 2002). Do actions for "Rub-A-Dub Dub" while sitting on the floor, then rock forward and backward pretending to row a boat for "Row, Row, Row Your Boat."

- Play the tune "Everybody Wash" on the sound recording *Splish Splash Bathtime Fun* by Sesame Street (Children's Television Workshop, 1995). Pretend to wash body parts such as ears, tummy, kneecaps, and thumbs as directed by Sesame Street characters Ernie and Bert.

- Play the tune "[Wash Your] Head, Shoulders, Knees, and Toes" on the sound recording *Bathtime Magic* by Joanie Bartels (Discovery Music, 2002). Pretend to wash each body part in turn in this engaging twist on the familiar "Head, Shoulders, Knees, and Toes."

- Read *King Bidgood's in the Bathtub* by Audrey Wood; illustrated by Don Wood (Harcourt, 1985). Despite pleas from his court, a fun-loving king refuses to get out of his bathtub to rule his kingdom. Lead the group in the repeated refrain: "King Bidgood's in the bathtub, and he won't get out! Oh, who knows what to do?"

- Make the shapes of "D" and "d" using string, pipe cleaners, or clay.

Rub-A-Dub Dub

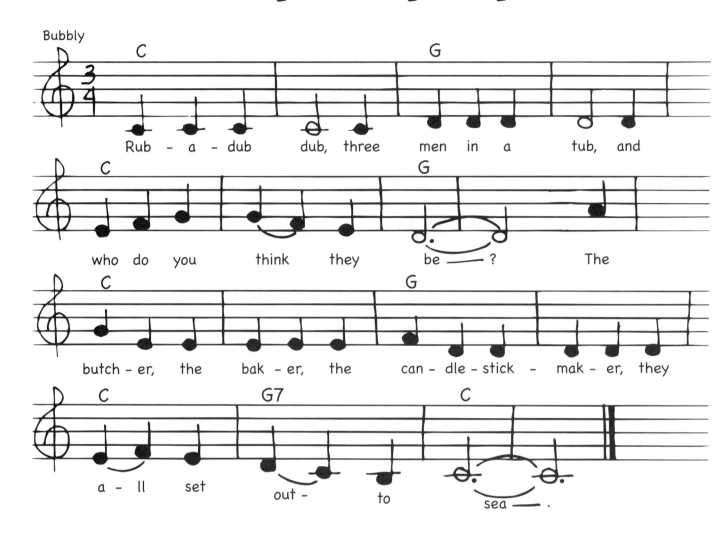

Bubbly

Rub - a - dub dub, three men in a tub, and who do you think they be ——? The butch - er, the bak - er, the can - dle - stick - mak - er, they a - ll set out - to sea ——.

Take-home Rub-A-Dub Dub

Rub-a-dub dub,

Three men in a tub,

And who do you think they be?

The butcher, the baker, the candlestick-maker,

They all set out to sea.

Bibliographies and Resources

Mother Goose Collections to Share and Recommend

Alderson, Brian (sel.). *Cakes and Custard.* William Morrow & Co., 1975, 1974.

Crews, Nina. *The Neighborhood Mother Goose.* Greenwillow Books, 2004.

dePaola, Tomie. *Tomie dePaola's Mother Goose.* Putnam, 1985.

Engelbreit, Mary. *Mary Engelbreit's Mother Goose: One Hundred Best-Loved Verses.* HarperCollins, 2005.

Foreman, Michael. *Michael Foreman's Mother Goose.* Harcourt, 1991.

Hoberman, Mary Ann. *You Read to Me, I'll Read to You: Very Short Mother Goose Tales to Read Together.* Little, Brown and Company, 2005.

Kubler, Annie, illus. *Pat-a-Cake!: Nursery Rhymes.* Child's Play, 2005. (Board book)

Kubler, Annie, illus. *Peek-a-Boo!: Nursery Games.* Child's Play, 2005. (Board book)

Kubler, Annie, illus. *See-Saw! Nursery Songs.* Child's Play, 2005. (Board book)

Lansky, Bruce. *Mary Had a Little Jam and Other Silly Rhymes.* Meadowbrook Press, 2004. Reprint of *The New Adventures of Mother Goose: Gentle Rhymes for Happy Times* (1993).

Lobel, Arnold. *Arnold Lobel's Book of Mother Goose.* Knopf, 1997. Reprint of *The Random House Book of Mother Goose* (1986).

Long, Sylvia. *Sylvia Long's Mother Goose.* Chronicle Books, 1999.

Opie, Iona, ed. Illus. by Rosemary Wells. *My Very First Mother Goose.* Candlewick Press, 1996.

Opie, Iona, ed. Illus. by Rosemary Wells. *Here Comes Mother Goose.* Candlewick Press, 1999.

Scarry, Richard. *Richard Scarry's Best Mother Goose Ever.* Western Publishing Co., 1970, 1964.

Smith, Jessie Willcox. *The Jessie Willcox Smith Mother Goose.* Derrydale Books, 1986.

Wright, Blanche Fisher, illus. *The Real Mother Goose.* Checkerboard Press, 1944, 1916.

Yaccarino, Dan, illus. *Dan Yaccarino's Mother Goose.* Random House, 2004.

History of Nursery Rhymes

Baring-Gould, William S., and Cecil Baring-Gould. *The Annotated Mother Goose.* Crown Publishers, 1962.

Christensen, James C. *Rhymes & Reasons: An Annotated Collection of Mother Goose Rhymes.* The Greenwich Workshop Press, 1977.

Delamar, Gloria T. *Mother Goose: From Nursery to Literature.* McFarland, 1987.

Montgomery, Michael G., and Wayne Montgomery. *Over the Candlestick: Classic Nursery Rhymes and the Real Stories Behind Them.* Peachtree Publishers, 2002.

Opie, Iona and Peter, eds. *The Oxford Dictionary of Nursery Rhymes.* Clarendon Press, 1951.

Roberts, Chris. *Heavy Words Lightly Thrown: The Reason Behind the Rhyme.* Gotham Books, 2005.

Stevens, Albert Mason. *The Nursery Rhyme: Remnant of Popular Protest.* Coronado Press, 1968.

Thomas, K. E. *The Real Personages of Mother Goose.* Lothrop, Lee & Shepard, 1930.

Mother Goose Crafts

Cressy, Judith. *What Can You Do with a Paper Bag? Hats, Wigs, Masks, Crowns, Helmets, and Headdresses.* Chronicle Books, 2001.

Renfro, Nancy, and Tamara Hunt. *A Pocketful of Puppets: Mother Goose.* Nancy Renfro Studios, 1982.

Ross, Kathy. *Crafts From Your Favorite Children's Songs.* Millbrook Press, 2001.

Ross, Kathy. *Crafts From Your Favorite Nursery Rhymes.* Millbrook Press, 2002.

Ross, Kathy. *Crafts to Make in the Spring.* Millbrook Press, 1998.

Mother Goose Songbooks

Barratt, Carol. *The Mother Goose Songbook: Nursery Rhymes to Play and Sing.* Arranged for the piano by Carol Barratt. Derrydale Books, 1984.

Beall, Pamela Conn, and Susan Hagen Nipp. *Wee Sing Nursery Rhymes & Lullabies.* Price Stern Sloan, 2005, 2002, 1985.

Buck, Sir Percy. *The Oxford Nursery Song Book.* 3d ed. Oxford University Press, 1984, 1961, 1933.

Crane, Walter. *The Baby's Bouquet.* Robert Frederick Ltd., 1994. (First published in 1877.)

Crane, Walter. *The Baby's Opera.* Simon & Schuster, 1981. (First published in 1879.)

Larrick, Nancy, comp. *Songs from Mother Goose: With the Traditional Melody for Each.* Harper & Row, 1989.

Orth, L. E. *Sixty Songs from Mother Goose.* Set to music by L. E. Orth. Oliver Ditson Company, 1906.

Rey, H. A. *Humpty Dumpty: And Other Mother Goose Songs.* HarperFestival, 1995.

Sharon, Lois & Bram's Mother Goose. Little, Brown and Company, 1985.

Yolen, Jane. *Jane Yolen's Mother Goose Songbook.* Boyds Mills Press, 1992.

Yolen, Jane, ed. *This Little Piggy: And Other Rhymes to Sing and Play.* [Music CD included.] Candlewick Press, 2005.

Sound Recordings

Beall, Pamela Conn, and Susan Hagen Nipp. *Wee Sing Nursery Rhymes & Lullabies.* Price Stern Sloan, 2005, 2002, 1985.

The Countdown Kids. *Mommy and Me: Mary Had a Little Lamb.* Mommy and Me Enterprises, 1998.

The Countdown Kids. *Mommy and Me: Old MacDonald Had a Farm.* Mommy and Me Enterprises, 1998.

The Countdown Kids. *Mommy and Me: Rock-a-bye Baby.* Mommy and Me Enterprises, 1998.

The Countdown Kids. *Mommy and Me: Twinkle Twinkle Little Star.* Mommy and Me Enterprises, 1998.

Feldman, Jean. *Nursery Rhymes and Good Ol' Times with Dr. Jean.* Jean Feldman, 2002.

Hegner, Priscilla A. *Baby Games (6 Weeks - 1 Year).* Kimbo Educational, 1987.

Hegner, Priscilla, and Rose Grasselli. *Diaper Gym: Fun Activities for Babies on the Move.* Kimbo Educational, 1985.

Hegner, Priscilla. *Teach a Toddler: Playful Songs for Learning.* Kimbo Educational, 1985.

Jenkins, Ella. *Early, Early Childhood Songs.* Smithsonian Folkways Recordings, 1990.

Jenkins, Ella. *Nursery Rhymes: Rhyming and Remembering.* Smithsonian Folkways Recordings, 1974.

McGrath, Bob. *If You're Happy & You Know It ... Sing Along with Bob #1.* Bob's Kids Music, 1996, 1990.

McGrath, Bob, and Katharine Smithrim. *The Baby Record.* Bob's Kids Music, 2000.

McGrath, Bob, and Katharine Smithrim. *Songs & Games For Toddlers.* Bob's Kids Music, 2000.

Palmer, Hap. *Early Childhood Classics: Old Favorites With A New Twist.* Hap-Pal Music, Inc., 2000.

Palmer, Hap. *Hap Palmer Sings Classic Nursery Rhymes.* Educational Activities, Inc., 2003; Hap-Pal Music, Inc., 1991.

Raffi. *Singable Songs for the Very Young*. Troubador Records Ltd., 1976.

Sharon, Lois & Bram. *Mainly Mother Goose: Songs and Rhymes For Merry Young Souls*. Elephant Records, 1984.

Snee, Richard. *Mother Goose Rocks! Volume 1*. Boffomedia, Inc., 2000.

Sunseri, Mary Lee. *Mother Goose Melodies: Four & Twenty Olde Songs for Young Children*. Piper Grove, 2003.

Spanish Language Resources

Ada, Alma Flor, and F. Isabel Campoy. *Mama Goose: A Latino Nursery Treasury; Un Tesoro De Rimas Infantiles*. Illus. by Maribel Suarez. English editing by Tracy Hefferman. Hyperion, 2004.

Ada, Alma Flor, and F. Isabel Campoy, sel. *¡Pio Peep!: Traditional Spanish Nursery Rhymes*. English adapt. by Alice Schertle. Illus. by Vivi Escriva. HarperCollins, 2003. (Book and CD set: Rayo, 2006.)

Carlson, Ann, and Mary Carlson, illus. *Flannelboard Stories for Infants and Toddlers*, Bilingual Edition (Spanish-English). American Library Assn., 2005.

Hall, Nancy Abraham, and Jill Syverson-Stork, sel. and adapt. *Los Pollitos Dicen: Juegos, Rimas y Canciones Infantiles de Países de Habla Hispana; The Baby Chicks Sing: Traditional Games, Nursery Rhymes, and Lullabies from Spanish-Speaking Countries*. Illus. by Kay Chorao. Little, Brown and Company, 1994.

Orozco, Jose-Luis, sel., arr., and transl. *De Colores: and Other Latin-American Folk Songs for Children*. Illus. by Elisa Kleven. Dutton, 1994.

Orozco, Jose-Luis. *Jose-Luis Orozco Canta De Colores* [sound recording]. Arcoiris Records, 1996.

Orozco, Jose-Luis, sel., arr., and transl. *Diez Deditos; Ten Little Fingers & Other Play Rhymes and Action Songs from Latin America*. Illus. by Elisa Kleven. Dutton, 1997.

Orozco, Jose-Luis. *Diez Deditos* [sound recording]. Arcoiris Records, 1997.

Orozco, Jose-Luis. *Rin, Rin, Rin; Do, Re, Mi*. Illus. by David Diaz. Scholastic, 2005.

Orozco, Jose-Luis. *Rin, Rin, Rin; Do, Re, Mi* [sound recording]. Arcoiris Records, 2005.

See Jose-Luis Orozco's Web site at www.joseluisorozco.com for the following sound recordings and more:

Orozco, Jose-Luis. *Lirica Infantil volume #1: Latin American Children's Songs, Games and Rhymes*. Arcoiris Records.

Orozco, Jose-Luis. *Lirica Infantil volume #2: Latin American Children's Songs, Games and Rhymes*. Arcoiris Records.

Orozco, Jose-Luis. *Lirica Infantil volume #3: Latin American Children's Songs, Games and Rhymes*. Arcoiris Records.

Where to Buy Sound Recordings

Arcoiris Records (Jose-Luis Orozco)
P.O. Box 461900
Los Angeles, CA 90046
888.354.7373 phone / 310.659.4144 fax
www.joseluisorozco.com

Educational Record Center
3233 Burnt Mill Drive, Suite 100
Wilmington, NC 28403-2698
888.372.4543 phone / 888.438.1637 fax
www.erckids.com

Kimbo Educational
P.O. Box 477 J
Long Branch, NJ 07740
800.631.2187 phone / 732.870.3340 fax
www.Kimboed.com

Music for Little People
P.O. Box 1460
Redway, CA 95560-1460
707.923.3991 phone / 800.409.2457 phone
www.musicforlittlepeople.com

Where to Buy Alphabet Letters

Childcraft Education Corp.
P. O. Box 3239
Lancaster, PA 17604
800.631.5652 phone / 888.532.4453 fax
www.childcraft.com
(Jumbo 4.7" high UPPERCASE Letters, item #5G358374; Jumbo 4.3" high LOWERCASE Letters, item #5G358382)

Constructive Playthings
13201 Arrington Road
Grandview, MO 64030-1117
800.448.4115 phone / 816.761.9295 fax
www.cptoys.com
(Giant 4.75" Magnetic Foam UPPERCASE
Letters, item #EDL-776; Giant 4.75" Magnetic
Foam LOWERCASE Letters, item #EDL-617)
(Jumbo 7.5" Foam UPPERCASE Letters, item
#EDL-170; Jumbo 7.25" Foam LOWERCASE
Letters, item #EDL-171)

Highsmith Inc.
W5527 State Road 106
P.O. Box 800
Fort Atkinson, WI 53538-0800
800.558.2110 phone / 800.835.2329 fax
www.highsmith.com
(Durafoam Letters—6", 8", 10", and 12" high)

Lakeshore Learning Materials
2695 E. Dominguez Street
Carson, CA 90895
800.778.4456 phone / 800.537.5403 fax
www.lakeshorelearning.com
(Jumbo 5" Magnetic Letters—UPPERCASE,
item #RR932; Jumbo 5" Magnetic Letters—
LOWERCASE, item #RR933)

Storybook and Sound Recording Titles Listed in *Mother Goose Rhyme Time: People*

Bartels, Joanie. *Bathtime Magic*. Discovery Music, 2002.

Brown, Margaret Wise. *Home for a Bunny*. Golden Books, 1988, 1984, 1960, 1956.

Ehlert, Lois. *Pie in the Sky*. Harcourt, 2004.

Ehlert, Lois. *Planting a Rainbow*. Harcourt, 1988.

Hale, Sarah Josepha. Photo illus. by Bruce McMillan. *Mary Had a Little Lamb*. Scholastic, 1990.

Hale, Sarah Josepha. Retold by Isa Trapani. *Mary Had a Little Lamb*. Whispering Coyote Press, 1998.

Hall, Zoe. *The Apple Pie Tree*. Scholastic, 1996.

Hoberman, Mary Ann (adapt.) *Mary Had a Little Lamb*. Little, Brown and Company, 2003.

Hoberman, Mary Ann. *You Read to Me, I'll Read to You: Very Short Mother Goose Tales to Read Together*. Little, Brown and Company, 2005.

Jeram, Anita. *Contrary Mary*. Candlewick Press, 1995.

Morris, Ann. *Houses and Homes*. Lothrop, Lee & Shepard Books, 1992.

Root, Phyllis. *The House that Jill Built*. Candlewick Press, 2005.

Sesame Street. *Splish Splash Bathtime Fun*. Children's Television Workshop, 1995.

Shaw, Nancy. *Sheep Take a Hike*. Houghton Mifflin, 1994.

Shaw, Nancy. *Sheep in a Jeep*. Houghton Mifflin, 1986.

Shaw, Nancy. *Sheep on a Ship*. Houghton Mifflin, 1989.

Shaw, Nancy. *Sheep in a Shop*. Houghton Mifflin, 1991.

Shaw, Nancy. *Sheep Out to Eat*. Houghton Mifflin, 1992.

Skorpen, Liesel Moak. *We Were Tired Of Living In a House*. Putnam, 1999.

Wood, Audrey. *King Bidgood's in the Bathtub*. Harcourt, 1985.

Mother Goose and Early Literacy Programming Books, Articles, and Video/DVDs

Briggs, Diane. *Toddler Storytime Programs*. Scarecrow Press, 1993.

Brown, Marc, coll. and illus. *Finger Rhymes*. Dutton, 1980.

Brown, Marc, coll. and illus. *Hand Rhymes*. Dutton, 1985.

Brown, Marc, coll. and illus. *Play Rhymes*. Dutton, 1987.

Butler, Dorothy. *Babies Need Books*. Atheneum, 1980.

Clow-Martin, Elaine. *Baby Games: The Joyful Guide to Child's Play from Birth to Three Years*. Rev. ed. Fitzhenry & Whiteside Ltd., 2003, Running Press, 1988.

Cobb, Jane. *I'm a Little Teapot! Presenting Preschool Storytime*. 2d ed. Black Sheep Pr., 1996.

Cobb, Jane. *What'll I Do with the Baby-oh? Nursery Rhymes, Songs and Stories for Babies*. Black Sheep Pr., 2006.

Cole, Joanna, and Stephanie Calmenson. *The Eentsy, Weentsy Spider; Fingerplays and Action Rhymes*. William Morrow, 1991.

Cole, Joanna, and Stephanie Calmenson. *Pat-A-Cake and Other Play Rhymes*. HarperCollins, 1992.

Davis, Robin Works. *Toddle On Over: Developing Infant & Toddler Literature Programs*. Alleyside Press, 1998.

De Salvo, Nancy. *Beginning with Books: Library Programming for Infants, Toddlers, and Preschoolers*. Library Professional Publications, 1993.

Diamant-Cohen, Betsy. "Mother Goose on the Loose: Applying Brain Research to Early Childhood Programs in the Public Library." *Public Libraries*, 43.1 (2004): 41–45.

Diamant-Cohen, Betsy, Ellen Riordan, and Regina Wade. "Make Way for Dendrites: How Brain Research Can Impact Children's Programming." *Children & Libraries*, 2.1 (2004): 12–20.

Diamant-Cohen, Betsy. *Mother Goose on the Loose*. Neal Schuman, 2006.

Ernst, Linda L. *Lapsit Services for the Very Young: A How-To-Do-It Manual*. Neal Schuman, 1995.

Ernst, Linda L. *Lapsit Services for the Very Young II: A How-To-Do-It Manual*. Neal Schuman, 2001.

Fehrenbach, Laurie A., and David P. Hurford, Carolyn R. Fehrenbach, and Rebecca Groves. "Developing the Emergent Literacy of Preschool Children through a Library Outreach Program." *Journal of Youth Services in Libraries*, 12:1 (1998): 40–1.

Ghoting, Saroj Nadkarni, and Pamela Martin-Diaz. *Early Literacy Storytimes @ Your Library: Partnering with Caregivers for Success*. American Library Assn., 2006.

Greene, Ellin. *Books, Babies, and Libraries*. American Library Assn., 1991.

Herb, Steve. "Building Blocks for Literacy: What Current Research Shows." *School Library Journal*, 43.7 (1997): 23.

Huebner, Colleen E. *Hear and Say Reading* [VHS or DVD]. Rotary Club of Bainbridge Island, 2001. (www.bainbridgeislandrotary.org)

Jeffery, Debby Ann. *Literate Beginnings: Programs for Babies and Toddlers*. American Library Assn., 1995.

Jeffery, Debby, and Ellen Mahoney. "Sitting Pretty: Infants, Toddlers, & Lapsits." *School Library Journal*, 35.8 (1989): 37–9.

Marino, Jane. "B Is for Baby, B Is for Books." *School Library Journal*, 43.3 (1997): 110–11.

Marino, Jane. *Babies in the Library!* Scarecrow Press, 2003.

Marino, Jane, and Dorothy F. Houlihan. *Mother Goose Time: Library Programs for Babies and Their Caregivers*. H. W., Wilson, 1992.

McGuiness, Diane. *Growing a Reader from Birth: Your Child's Path from Language to Literacy*. W. W. Norton & Co., 2004.

Nespeca, Sue McLeaf. "Bringing Up Baby." *School Library Journal*, 45, no. 11 (November 1999): 48-52.

Nespeca, Sue McLeaf. *Library Programming for Families with Young Children: A How-to-Do-It Manual*. Neal Schuman, 1994.

Neuman, Susan B. ed., et al. *Access for All: Closing the Book Gap for Children in Early Education*. International Reading Association, 2001.

Newcome, Zita. *Head, Shoulders, Knees, and Toes; and Other Action Rhymes*. Candlewick Press, 2002.

Nichols, Judy. *Storytimes for Two-Year-Olds*. 2d ed. American Library Assn., 1998.

Silberg, Jackie, and Pam Schiller, compilers. *The Complete Book of Rhymes, Songs, Poems, Fingerplays and Chants*. Gryphon House, 2002.

Walter, Virginia A. *Output Measures for Public Library Service to Children: A Manual of Standardized Procedures*. American Library Assn., 1992.

Wilner, Isabel, sel. *The Baby's Game Book*. Illus. by Sam Williams. Greenwillow Books, 2000.

Winkel, Lois, and Sue Kimmel. *Mother Goose Comes First: An Annotated Guide to the Best Books and Recordings for Your Preschool Child.* Henry Holt & Company, 1990.

Mother Goose Programming and Early Literacy Web Connections

America Reads Challenge
www.ed.gov/inits/americareads/index.html

Association of Library Service to Children: Born to Read: How to Raise a Reader
www.ala.org/ala/alsc/alscresources/bornto read/bornread.htm

Champaign Public Library (IL): Just for Kids: Mother Goose
www.champaign.org/kids/mgoose_tips.html

Children of the Code
www.childrenofthecode.org

Early Literacy and Brain Development Resources (Saroj Ghoting)
www.earlylit.net/earlylit/bibliography.html

Every Child Ready to Read @ Your Library
www.pla.org/earlyliteracy.htm

Hennepin County Library (MN): Birth to Six
www.hclib.org/BirthTo6/

Mother Goose Society
www.librarysupport.net/mothergoosesociety/

Multnomah County (OR) Public Library: Early Words
www.multcolib.org/birthtosix/

National Association of Education for the Young Child
www.naeyc.org/

Nursery Rhymes at the Virtual Vine
www.thevirtualvine.com/nurseryrhymes.html

Project ECLIPSE: Mother Goose
eclipse.rutgers.edu/goose/literacy/

Public Library of Charlotte & Mecklenburg County: Grow & Learn @ Your Library
www.plcmc.org/forKids/growlearn/

Reading Is Fundamental (RIF)
www.rif.org

A Rhyme a Week: Nursery Rhymes for Early Literacy
curry.edschool.virginia.edu/go/wil/rimes_ and_rhymes.htm

West Bloomfield Township Public Library (MI): Grow Up Reading @ the West Bloomfield Township Public Library
www.growupreading.org

Zero to Three's Brain Wonders
www.zerotothree.org/brainwonders/